No F
In T

by Colin Heathcote

Mum,

Xmas 2017

your loving son and future daughter in law,

Simon + Holly xx

Copyright © 2015 Colin Heathcote

All rights reserved.

ISBN:
ISBN-13:978-1519174567
ISBN-10:151917456X

This book is dedicated to the ever-diminishing band of professional reporters and photographers working on the UK's remaining local weekly and regional daily newspapers.

Colin Heathcote was born and educated in Watford. After leaving school he worked At Watford Magistrates' Court and Television Audience Measurement (TAM) Ltd in Berkhamsted before being taken on as a junior reporter at the Berkhamsted Gazette.

Following his work as a local weekly newspaper journalist, he embarked on a PR career in local government with Hackney Council, Hampshire County Council and finally Northumberland County Council.

After retiring in 1995 he set up as a freelance PR consultant working with local and regional companies, organisations and charities. He currently works part time for Barking Mad, the home from home dog care specialists.

His interests include amateur dramatics and community radio broadcasting.

He lives with his wife, Pru, an author, playwright and creative writing tutor, in Warkworth, Northumberland. The couple have three children - Ben, Selina and Anna - and a grandchild, Sophie.

After an ill-judged and wholly unsuccessful attempt at getting a first book published in the late 1960s, he decided to let the dust die before trying again in 2015.

No Fires In Tring

Paul Barnes is a 21-year-old aspiring journalist who, after leaving school with a couple of O levels five years earlier, finally lands a job as a reporter with the Berkhamsted Gazette, part of Hertfordshire Newspapers Ltd.

Whilst the obtaining of the newspaper stories has been embellished for (hopefully) comic effect, the recorded articles in the following chapters are as appeared in the Gazette. The characters featured are based on people who worked for the company, although their names have been changed.

'No Fires In Tring' is a fictionalised account of life on a rural local weekly newspaper in the mid to late 1960s; a world which has long since disappeared. Since those days many dozens of small weekly and regional daily papers in the UK have disappeared to be replaced by free papers, news web sites and information churning social media networks. The local offices of the Berkhamsted Gazette, Tring and District News and Hemel Hempstead Gazette have been closed; the papers are no longer produced in the county of Hertfordshire but in Aylesbury, Buckinghamshire.

A career in weekly or regional newspaper journalism or photography is now open to comparatively few young people as papers increasingly source their 'news' and pictures from the public and PR practitioners.

Chapter 1

"Are you gregariush?"

I looked at him intently. Maintain eye contact; that's the important thing. One of the first rules for those trying to make an impression is to establish a rapport. That's what I had been told. It helps to establish a bond….to ensure that a mental impact is made.

Harry Symonds, with cigar in hand, sat sprawled in a big leather armchair and behind a huge oak table that was littered with scraps of yellowish copy paper of approximately A5 size. He was a man of about 55 with a full head of greying wavy hair and a thinnish moustache which had not quite given up being black but was clearly in no mood to fight the discolouring that advancing years brings. He looked overweight and the dim light of the office was insufficient to properly expose the full glory of his mottled red and blue nose.

There was a certain whiff in the office that Saturday afternoon in early June. As a 21-year-old with some experience of pubs and bars, my olfactory senses were reasonably well developed, and I could detect a distinct alcoholic element. I wouldn't say that it was unpleasant, but what was it….?

Hang on, he's just asked me a question and I haven't a bloody clue what 'gregarious' means. It's time to panic. Now, come on….don't display your ignorance by asking him what it means. Take a chance. Go for it.

"Er…no. But I like to think I'm a good mixer."

I searched his face for some kind of acknowledgement to my response. Nothing really. Must have struck lucky. Hey, who's a clever boy then?

I'd always wanted to be a journalist. Even at Vics (Victoria, a boys' secondary modern school in Addiscombe Road, Watford) I had visions of joining the 'made an excuse and left' school of investigative journalism. Although I'd written to most of the national dailies without getting a reply when I was 16, I still hoped that one day I'd get a chance to join a paper. And here I was, in the office of the Editor of the Berkhamsted Gazette, talking to the great man who was going to give me some words of wisdom about what I should do.

Fed up with working for Television Audience Measurement (TAM) Ltd, which was based in the town, I'd decided to have another crack at realising my ambition to become a journalist. So I had telephoned the Editor of the Gazette for advice on how I might break into the profession. He told me to write a local story and send it in and he would have a look at it. He was non-specific about the subject matter, saying that he'd consider anything provided it was of local interest.

Well, that's a start. At least I had managed to speak to someone in the business.

Having worked in the town for a couple of years I was familiar with the surroundings and, in particular, its many watering holes.

'That's it...I'll do a story about the pubs of Berkhamsted,' I thought. 'I'll emphasise the quantity and quality of the licensed premises that litter the town.'.

I duly wrote the piece after undertaking some fairly intensive research and product sampling, and sent it in. A couple of weeks went by without response. So I rang up and again spoke to Harry Symonds. It took a bit of time and a long explanation before he realised what I was going on about.

"What did you think of the story, Mr Symonds?" I asked.

There was a pause and I could hear a rustling of papers.

"Yes...yes. It, um, shows a certain amount of flair. Come in and we'll talk about it."

Wow...what a result. He clearly felt I had some talent. This was a real ego boost for me. Now perhaps he'll be able to give me some worthwhile advice.

"When shall I come in?"

"Saturday afternoon. Three o clock. Don't be late."

"Right. Thank you. Thank you...."

By now I was talking to myself. He'd hung up.

Two days later and only fifteen minutes after the scheduled appointment time I strolled into his office. And here was Harry was looking at my story. (Didn't know then that stories were 'copy'). He was reading it aloud - or at least parts of it, as if he was selecting the key points…or was it the crap bits. The room was warming up in the early summer sunshine and again I could feel my attention wandering. The window looked out on to a small patch of recently mown grass and beyond to an almost empty car park. 'Christ, that's alright,' I thought as a young mini-skirted vision tripped her way towards an ageing Morris Minor. I could just make out the line of her considerable chest if I rocked slightly back in the chair. 'Wheey, look at the size of…'. My fantasy drew to an abrupt halt as the chair screeched back to an upright position on the polished oak floor.

"What, what…!?" The Editor and I released the exclamations in unison.

Harry Symonds opened his eyes. He blinked and went to default position of studiously examining the bits of paper in front of him.

"Er....um...sorry," he said. "I think I must have dozed off. It's been a long day. I've been very busy."

He had actually fallen asleep whilst scanning my terrifically interesting story about the town's many and varied public houses. (There are a lot – even now; so worth a visit). There was a telltale rivulet of dribble running down the side of his mouth and a damp patch on my copy.

 "So…..what do you think of it, Mr Symonds?"

"Uh?"

"Uh...the story."

"What?"

"The…um, the story that I wrote. Does it read ok."

"Story?"

What is going on? It's definitely there in his hand, but I can't tell him that. I'll have to get round it somehow.

"Yes, I wrote a piece about the fine inns and public houses of Berkhamsted and asked if you could take a look at it and give me your opinion."

"Did you? I don't recall….oh now you come to mention it I have seen it somewhere. It must be in my bag."

He put my story down on the table and started to rifle through bits of paper in the bulky brief case that lay at his feet. His hand kept knocking against what sounded like a couple of bottles.

This could be a long afternoon, I thought. As he was bending down I reached over and took the collection of handwritten sheets he had been holding. He came up from his semi-prone position and saw the papers in my hand.

"Is that the story?"

"Er….yes….it is."

"Well give it to me. I can hardly give you an opinion about your work if you keep hold of it."

"Right. Er…of course."

"Now…..let me see."

He started to read the piece again.

"This looks familiar……are you sure you haven't copied this from somewhere?"

By now I was beginning to panic again. Had I imagined the past twenty minutes or so? No, I distinctly remember walking into the room and his question about my gregariousness or gregariocity or whatever the word is for someone who is gregarious.

"No. Honestly. It's what I wrote. I didn't copy anything."

I felt like I was making the type of excuse that was my trademark at school when any ridiculous lie was employed to extricate myself from an awkward situation. Only this time, it was true. I had written it myself…every word of it. My research had been pretty exhaustive. Maybe it wasn't to be my day after all.

"Hmm," he said, a tad grumpily.

A few more embarrassing minutes passed and he suddenly got up with the story and walked out of the room.

"Back in a minute….nature calls."

This was not going well. Perhaps if I just left now, I could get back in time to hear some of the cricket….or whip round to the car park to see if the vision is still around. Maybe her car won't start and she's bending over the engine and you can see her tits…I could offer to help, and she'd be soooh grateful that she'd invite me back to her place and I'd say ok and the moment we were inside her flat, she'd be all over me and……the fantasy ended as I heard what sounded like a glass clinking. What *is* he doing in there? I heard a cistern flush, a door swing open and his steps on the tiled floor outside the office. He re-emerged into the room.

"Hello. Who are you?"

"Pardon?"

"I shed who…who are you?"

Bloody hell. He's pissed. How could he have got pissed in the two minutes that he'd been gone?

"I'm Paul Barnes, Mr Symonds….I'm the one you told to come in this afternoon. You were looking at the story I wrote."

"Washtorry….I haven't sheen a shtorry. Washit about?

It really was time to go.

"Perhaps I'd better go Mr Symonds. You're obviously very…..um very occupied. Being an editor must be a very…er... very taxing job and you're probably very busy. It was good of you to see me."

"I'm always bizzhy…an editor hash to be on hish toesh at all timesh. What wash your name again?"

"Barnes…Paul Barnes."

"Well, Paul….you sheem jush the short of chap we need. Can you shtart Monday? Nine o'clock."

"What…you're offering me the job? I wasn't expecting….I mean, I er, I accept of course. That's great. Absolutely marvellous Thanks. Thanks a lot."

If I hadn't said so much, I would have been speechless. I had been offered the job of a reporter on a paper.

"You're very welcome….now do you have a car?"

"Er…yes. So there won't be any problem getting out and about in the area. It's fairly dependable (it wasn't, but this wasn't the time to go into detail) I've got a clean licence and……"

"Ish it nearby?"

"It's parked in that car park at the bottom of the garden."

"Jolly good."

"Em…er. Is it?"

"Yesh."

"Whysh that?" Christ, he's got me at it now. "Er. I mean, why is it jolly good?"

"Cosh I need you to do shumshing for me."

Blimey. I've only just been offered a job and he already wants me to go out on a story. Hope it's a major crime. Or maybe a sex scandal. Hey this day is getting better all the time. Wait a minute. I haven't got a notebook or pencil. Shit, I'll have to ask him for them…he won't think that's very professional. Oh, well, here goes.

"Er…can I borrow some paper and a pencil……um….you know, to take notes. Can you give me one or two details…um…any contact names?"

"What?"

"Er…names. You know, um…of people who might be able to give me details …you know fill me in about the story."

"Washstorry?"

Is this what they call deja vu? "You said that you wanted me to do something and so I was wondering what..who..?"

I looked at him closely and his eyes were beginning to shut. It can't be…no, surely I'm imagining it. Hell's teeth, he's nodded off again. What should I do? I know, I'll cough.

"eruggh, eruggh" I spluttered.

Nothing. He was well away.

"ERUGGH, ERUGGH…."

This wasn't working. What the bloody hell do I do now? I leant over and prodded him in the shoulder. His head lolled slightly. And his eyes opened.

"Oh… what…er…jush a small one then...eh?"

"Mr Symonds, you said you wanted me to do something…"

"Ish time I wasshunt here….are you from Town Taxshees? You're not my ushawl driver."

I'd heard of parallel universes, but this was ridiculous. It was clear that I was not going to get any sense out of him in his state. Time to take control of the situation.

"No, I'm new. Only just started. Where to?

Chapter 2

I can't believe it. My first day. I hadn't looked forward to a Monday so much since the start of the summer holidays when I was at school. I wonder what kind of stories I'll be sent out to do. Probably won't get a real biggie on the first day....give myself a couple of days to learn the ropes and then go all out for an awe-inspiring scoop...a real exclusive....journos from all over will enviously ask how I did it....and isn't there something call the Pulitzer prize for best stories.....I can see it now, walking up to receive the award from, hmm, who might it be? Someone like Harold Wilson or Ted Heath or Bobby Charlton. I wouldn't be too pleased if it was the Queen, especially bearing in mind my anti-royalist attitudes, but, I suppose I'd have to swallow my pride and accept ...on behalf of journalism and ...

"Oi you twat...watch where you're going!"

Shit..."er..sorry." I looked apologetically towards the cyclist who was scrambling to control his bike on the grass verge onto which he'd been forced by my sit-up-and-beg Ford Anglia. I carefully drove along the high street or 'my patch' as I'll probably start calling it and turned right, down past the post office and into the car park behind the Gazette office. As I got out of the car, my stomach started to churn. This was it. The start of a new career. I walked out of the car park and back along the high street towards the Gazette office. It was nearly nine. Best to be a couple of minutes early on my first day. I expect the other reporters will be buzzing around, furiously typing away as they jam the 'phones between their ears talking to contacts. The editor will be barking out instructions above the hubbub....I reached the green door with the number 278 on it and turned the handle and...hang on, it's locked. Can't be, surely...I peered through the Venetian blinds hanging against the window and could see nothing. Where the hell was everyone….maybe they're all out on a big emergency… perhaps a multiple pile-up on the A41…..a barge collision on the Grand Union Canal. No, it must be a train crash.

"Won't be anybody there for at least 20 minutes!"

"Eh?"

"You must be a newcomer to the area. The office doesn't normally open up much before twenty past. Janet'll be in by then."

I looked into the face of a man in his thirties who was about to enter the premises next door – a firm of undertakers.

"Janet?"

"Yes, Janet. She looks after the advertising. Did you want to place an ad?"

"Er, no. I'm due to start my new job here….as a reporter."

"Ah. I heard they were getting somebody to take over from Davey. I'm Fred Hetherington. I'm sure we'll be meeting in a day or two."

"I hadn't planned on kicking the bucket that soon."

"Very good….most amusing. No, you'll be after names and stuff for obits."

"Obits? What are obits?"

"Obituaries. You know. Details of the deceased, information about the funeral….that sort of thing."

My heart sank. Death notices…details of funerals. Doesn't sound like the sort of thing a thrusting young journo like me would have to do. Ah, well. He seemed a likable enough bloke, but he probably doesn't know anything about the world of journalism, so I won't take issue with him.

"Ah, thanks Fred. Oh, I'm Paul. Paul Barnes."

I shook his hand.

"Well, Paul. Welcome to Berkhamsted."

He disappeared into the undertakers and I was left wondering what to do. I wandered up towards the traffic lights and in to the town centre and gazed absentmindedly at the shop windows. I looked at the clock on what appeared to be the town hall. Quarter to four. Perhaps I should treat myself to a watch from my first week's wages. I read the notices of meetings on the display board, but didn't really take anything in; my excitement was mounting. Oh, come on…it must be about twenty past by now.

I ambled back and reached the office just as a lady, presumably Janet, was unlocking the door. A pleasant faced shortish woman in her forties, she barely glanced back at me as I said 'hello'.

She looked me up and down. "Who are you?"

"Er…I'm Paul Barnes. Mr Symonds said I was to turn up at nine o'clock."

"What for?"

What for…*what for*? What does she mean, what for?

"Well, I'm a journalist…and I'm due to start working here today."

I somehow regretted referring to myself as a journalist, but I was a bit riled at this woman's attitude.

"So you're the new boy?" she said as she unlocked the door.

Boy....*boy*. I was outraged. I am a 21-year-old man with the beginnings of some very promising sideburns if you don't bloody mind. Cheek.

"Er…yes. Paul Barnes."

"Huh, typical. Nobody tells me anything. And why the silly old sod told you to be here for nine is beyond me. He never gets in much before ten and neither do the others. Well, come on. I'll show you where the coffee's kept. Mine's white without, tah very much. Milk should just about be ok."

Mine's white without….Christ what's going on? I'm not a bloody tea boy. I'm a journ…reporter, ok junior reporter.

"Um..ok."

I followed her out to a small lobby between the office and a single WC. The lobby had a sink, above which was a tile-clad ledge full of stained mugs. A jar of Maxwell House stood next to a bag of sugar complete with brown soggy lumps and a salt cellar. Janet reached into the sink where a half full bottle of milk stood inside a bowl of water. She sniffed the milk.

"It's ok…but you'll have to get a fresh bottle later on."

I found the electric kettle, filled it and plugged it in. The nerves that I had felt thirty minutes earlier had been replaced by a slight feeling of despondency. Making coffee in a pokey lobby next to the bog, which whiffed a bit of cigars, gas, damp, and stale urine wasn't quite how I pictured my introduction to the world of journalism when I drove in that warm June morning. I took the coffees out into the office where Janet was opening mail at her desk, which also served as the public reception counter.

"Where do I sit?"

Janet pointed to a small desk with a couple of drawers and a few paper clips strewn about its surface. I sat down and started to drink.

"Er, Janet. Can I call you Janet?"

"It's the only name I've got."

"Who else works here? Apart from Mr Symonds, of course."

"Clive and Chrissy. Chrissy'll be the first one in."

"How about Clive?"

"He'll be in much later. He'll be out doing his Tring calls." As she said this, a slight grin lightened her previous dour countenance. I was about to ask her what was funny but decided against it.

Chapter 3

A few minutes passed with me pretending to read a Berkhamsted Urban District Council committee report, which included the budget for a cemetery, that Janet had tossed over with a curt 'read that – you'll probably have to cover that meeting tonight'. Tonight....*tonight!* Nobody mentioned spending a night listening to doubtless worthy men and women discuss the merits of by-monthly grass cutting round the council-run last resting place of local residents. I mean, who gives a toss about the maintenance of graves? After all, once people are dead, they're dead. Hardly expect one of the cadavers to pop his head out of a plot and whinge about the bind weed sprouting like there's no tomorrow.- which, let's face it, for the dead, there isn't.

Janet cut into my gloom.

"One of the main reasons why people buy the Gutsache is to read about people who've snuffed it; it's the nature of this place."

I tried to focus again on the costing estimates for the mower service and the re-creosoting of the lock-up tool shed, but it was heavy going. Fortunately Chrissy – I assumed it was she – breezed into the office with a fag dangling from her glossed red lips.

She peered over her glasses at me.

"Er. Hello," I said. "I'm Paul...er Paul Barnes."

"Yes. *And?* "

What did she mean 'and'?

"Em...and er..and I'm pleased to meet you?"

"No, darling….what are you doing sitting at that desk?"

I didn't like this type of inquisition. Quite frankly I thought she was being rude. And, of course, mouth engaged several minutes before brain cranked into action.

"Well, if you want to know, I was just catching up on the latest exciting instalment of the on-going Berkhamsted Urban District Council run cemetery adventure tale, and I have reached a potentially explosive twist concerning the financing of mower servicing and boy, I can't wait to find out what happens when I ….."

Her sudden smile and my brain catching up caused me to pause.

"My query, darling, is more about your presence in the office."

"Oh, sorry. I suppose I'm a bit nervous what with it being my first day and everything. I'm the new reporter. Mr Symonds told me to report for duty this morning."

Chrissy Walker was about 28, tall, slim with longish legs, shortish black skirt and reddish hair. Not bad really, although the horn rimmed specs gave her something of a schoolmarm look.

"Report for duty…I like that. Well, Paul, your first duty is to get me a coffee…black without."

Again, her winning smile broke through my defensive bolshiness. There was something about the way she demanded the beverage that put me at my ease. I set forth to make the coffee as she continued talking to me.

"Have you done any newspaper work before?"

"A little bit." This was something of an exaggeration. Relief paper-round work at Green's newsagents in Watford was probably not what she was thinking of. "But, I'm keen to get stuck in. I've always wanted to be a journo."

"A *what*? You've always wanted to be a *what*?"

"Er…journo. You know, short for journalist…"

"I know what it means, darling. If I were you I would forget about describing yourself as that and stick to calling yourself a trainee reporter."

I brought the coffee to her desk. "There you are, white with two sugars."

Chrissy sighed and rolled her eyes upward and glanced over to Janet. "This boy's got a lot to learn."

After I had remade her drink to the correct recipe she pulled her chair next to mine. "The silly old bugger never mentioned your starting today. He never said anything even about holding interviews. When did he see you?"

"I came in on Saturday afternoon."

"Bloody Hell…was he sober?" She laughed and again looked at Janet.

"Er…well…um.."

"Only teasing, darling. It's just that his afternoons are usually spent in an alcoholic haze. I suppose you must have been the last one."

"The last one?"

"Candidate, darling. The last candidate."

"What candidates? I didn't know there were candidates."

"Come with me darling." She grabbed my hand and marched me towards the editor's office. "We'll soon get to the bottom of this.

She walked into the room where I had sat on Saturday. She opened the big wide drawer that faced Mr Symonds' chair.

"Just as I thought! Look."

She held aloft a wad of forms.

"Don't you realise what these are? They're application forms."

"Application forms?"

"Yes. They're application forms from people who applied for the job."

"What job?"

"Your job, you daft sod. Your job."

"But I didn't apply…"

"Didn't apply? Well how come you came in on Saturday?

"I only came in to ask for advice. I didn't know there was a job going…."

"Didn't know there was a….Christ, it's been advertised in the paper for the past four months. How couldn't you have known? Look."

She opened the current week's paper and found the sits vac columns. "There….read that!"

Sure enough, the advertisement, originally appearing on February 25 and running consecutively every week until June 17, two weeks after I was 'appointed', stated: "Applications are invited from a young man or a young lady to take up a career in journalism, GCE 'O' level English Language essential; shorthand and typing an advantage – Please apply in writing to the News Editor 'The Berkhamsted Gazette' 278 High Street, Berkhamsted."

"Er…I er hadn't actually read the paper and I don't come from round here. I just thought that he must have considered me to be, you know, a natural."

"Let me ask you something Paul. Have you got 'O' level English?"

"Well, actually, I've got both 'O' and 'A' levels in English. And I've got Economic Geography 'A' level." That should shut her up.

"Yes, marvellous, I'm sure. What about shorthand?…..Typing?"

"A bit." This was, in fact, true, as I had learnt the rudiments of both in a previously unsuccessful attempt to become a magistrates' court clerk's assistant.

"100 wpm and 35 wpm?"

"Er…wpm?"

"Words per minute, darling. Words per minute."

"Well, er, no. Not quite that quick." In truth it was more like, respectively, 10 and 3.5 wpm.

"Well, Mr journo Barnes, most of these applicants, who read the paper and who actually took the time and trouble to complete and send in application forms, have got decent shorthand and typing. Do you know what I think?"

I felt myself redden as it dawned on me what she was driving at.

"No," I lied.

"He hasn't interviewed anybody but you. We'd been on at him for ages to get the post filled but he was either too idle or too pissed to do anything about it. But you walk in on a Saturday afternoon having not filled in any forms or even seen the bloody paper, and walk out with the job 'cos he couldn't be arsed to do anything about organising interviews."

She looked at me as it hit home that I wouldn't have stood a chance of landing the job in a fair contest.

"Oh, no. What do you think he's going to do?" By now any remnants of confidence had disappeared and I was on the verge of tears. She came to my rescue.

"Do? *Do* ? Don't worry darling. He won't DO anything. He can hardly admit to being pissed when he hired you, can he? And, who knows, you may turn out to be a good reporter."

I searched into her gaze desperately hoping that I wouldn't detect an unsaid 'but I doubt it'. I inwardly sighed with relief at the absence of any such silent aside.

Chapter 4

Chrissy plonked more sets of urban and rural council committee minutes down on my desk (In the 1960s the urban district council looked after the town of Berkhamsted while the rural district was responsible for many of the services in the outlying villages and hamlets. Hertfordshire County Council was, and is, the authority responsible for social services, schools, major highways work, libraries and the fire brigade).

"There. You can be getting on with that lot while you wait for the old fool to get in...."

I still couldn't quite come to terms with her attitude to the Editor of the Gazette, but I refrained from comment.

"I've circled about half a dozen of the reports and decisions of various committees. Some we'll have already covered, but see if you can make any stories from them. Don't just copy what's there. Pick out the most interesting bits and maybe see if there's any potential in following them up. Oh, and stick a headline on them. Do you think you can manage that?"

"Yes."

"Where's your typewriter?"

"Eh?"

"Your typewriter…for knocking out copy."

"I haven't got one."

Chrissy let out one of those sighs which would become all too familiar in the days ahead.

"Surely to God you've got a typewriter. I mean how the hell did you think you were going hammer out the stories?"

"I thought it would be supplied."

"'Fraid not darling. You'll have to get yourself one. I'll see if anyone over at Hemel has got one to flog. In the meantime, use Clive's." She pointed to a smart compact Remington on the adjoining desk. "Here's some copy paper."

As I slid the paper into the roller, I felt a frisson of something akin to excitement. This was going to be my first story as a journalist. I felt I was at the start of something special. It was quite historic really. Now let's see what I can get my teeth into. Hmm… repainting of the Kings Road public toilets…um, proposal to change the servicing schedule of the street cleaning vehicles to every eighteen months rather than annually….Hmm...how about this one ? Its a recommendation to defer the decision for changing the colour scheme for doors and windows at the council's rent and rates office. Wow, what a choice. Gloomily I started to tap out bits from the report about the toilets:

The building maintenance committee of the Berkhamsted Urban District Council has recommended that the public toilets in Kings Road should be repainted in the forthcoming financial year 1967/68 and that the district council treasurer be advised to allocate appropriate funding for the task.

Hmm…not bad. Covered the important points. My first story. Ok, so it won't win an award, but I'm on my way. Now what about a headline ? I know, 'RECOMMENDATION TO RE-PAINT PUBLIC TOILETS'.

"How's this Chrissy?" I handed over the copy.

She read it out loud and finished with a bout of silly snoring noises.

"Well?"

"Bloody hell, Paul...only if I had difficulty getting off to sleep, would I read this. It's so boring. It's about public loos for Christ's sake. Do it again and try and be a bit inventive...you know, work in references to spending pennies or being caught short. There's bags of humour potential in this story. Remember a local newspaper's supposed to entertain as well as inform."

Right. She's asked for it. I'll give her humour. I started to type:

Visitors and residents seeking relief will not be able to use Kings Road toilets when the district council closes them for repainting next year. They'll have to clench their bottoms and cross their legs instead of being able to do their business.

The council will probably be spending lots of pennies on the building if the recommendation to repaint is approved. The district treasurer will work out how much and hopefully the council will pass a motion to get the work done.

It's not known whether council employees will carry out the job on piss work.

Now, what about a funny headline? 'BOGS CLOSED FOR WEE WHILE' Perhaps not. 'FLUSHED WITH COLOUR'? Hmm. How about 'NO POOS LOOS' Ah, yes that's a winner.

I casually passed the finished piece to Chrissy. "I think you'll find this fits the bill."

She stared at my copy with what didn't appear to be admiration. Her mouth opened as she rehearsed some of my clever puns. Finally she put it down with a slight shake of her head. Clearly she was not very impressed.

I was about to remonstrate when Mr Symonds marched into the office wearing a huge trench coat with a belt almost up by his chest and clutching a brown briefcase. I instinctively stood up as he caught my gaze. There seemed to be absolutely no sign of recognition of me.

"Er, good morning, Mr Symonds."

"Who are you?" he demanded.

Before I could answer, Janet chipped in: "He's Paul Barnes, remember. You appointed him on Saturday…you know, the new trainee reporter."

I stared at him as he struggled to remember his actions of two days before. He clearly could not recall anything. "Ah, yes…Peter…of course…er come in, and I'll brief you about what you'll be doing."

"Paul."

"Eh?"

"It's Paul."

"Of course it is…that's what I said. Come on."

I followed him to his room. It smelt of booze and stale cigar smoke. He sat heavily into his chair as I stood at the table. "Sit down, Peter…it is Peter, isn't it?"

"Paul."

"Sorry, Paul. Now, where's your application form?" He started to rummage in the sheaf of papers that Chrissy had held aloft earlier. "I had it here, I'm sure…"

"Mr Symonds, I don't think you'll….you'll." I stopped talking as brain started to engage. Keep your trap shut, Paul. He'll just think he's mislaid it. Fortunately he had not registered what I was saying and continued to fumble through the papers. Finally he stuffed them in his draw. "Oh, well they'll turn up later. Now, Peter.."

"Paul!"

"….Paul. I'm going to take you under my wing and make you into a first class reporter. But you've got to work hard and take heed of what I say. I used to work for the Express you know. Beaverbrook used to insist that I do the big stories. I was a war correspondent once. I was the first reporter to go into the Belsen concentration camp. Shocking, shocking. But that was what being a reporter was all about. I had to be ready for anything and everything. I was in the first tank to reach Dachau.. er…Belsen. Where was I? Oh yes, Peter, now, you won't be doing the big stories here to start with, but that doesn't stop you keeping your eyes and ears open, because news is happening all the time."

"Yes, Mr Symonds. I'm keen to learn. Chrissy has given me some council reports to look through and find stories."

"Good, good. Now, I've got a little job for you."

Ooh, great. Something I can get my teeth into. Get me away from those boring reports. "Right you are. What do you want me to do?"

He got out his wallet and produced a five-pound note. "Pop across to 'The George' and get five Castellas and a half bottle of Gordon's."

"Um, er, ok." I took the money and started to walk to the door.

"Wait a minute, you'll need this." He handed over the big leather briefcase.

"No. It's ok Mr Symonds. I'm sure I can manage without a bag."

"No. You will take it and you will put the gin and cigars in it and you will secure the straps of the bag before you leave the pub. Is that understood?"

"Er...yes. Right."

I took the briefcase, and walked out.

"You off to 'The George' for his daily provisions?" queried Janet.

"Yes. But he says I've got to take his briefcase. Can't understand why."

"He thinks that if you have the briefcase, nobody'll know what's going on. As if anybody is that bothered. They all know about him."

Sure enough as I walked into the public bar with the briefcase, the man behind the bar spotted me and asked if I was new and was I to take delivery of Mr Symonds' order. I nodded, and he reached for the cigars and gin, which he had already placed under the bar. He put them into the briefcase, took the fiver and gave me the change.

"See you tomorrow," he said cheerily.

Chapter 5

Later that morning, Clive breezed in and noisily sat down. After I had told him who I was, he reached over, shook my hand and introduced himself. Clive Gainsborough was a product of the town's big public school for boys. He was 20, a bit tubby, as tall as me – around six foot – and had a big open face which exuded humour.

"So this is your first job in journalism, is it Paul? What kept you?"

"Three wasted years as a clerk's clerk's assistant clerk at Watford Magistrates Court and a two-year spell at Television Audience Measurement here in Berkhamsted."

"Oh, yes. TAM. I know them. We've had a couple of stories about viewing figures and the odd puff about new appointments. So what made you leave them for us? It surely couldn't have been for the money."

Indeed it wasn't. My salary as a 21-year-old trainee journalist was, because pay scales were based on bands round centres of population and Berkhamsted being on the outer band of a small population centre, probably amongst the lowest in the land for my age.

"I always wanted to be a journalist; ever since I left school."

"Well, why the hell did you come here!?" He snorted with laughter.

Chrissy, who was the chief reporter cut into our conversation. "Clive, did you pick up anything during your Tring calls?"

"This and that."

"What, precisely? Any crimes? What about fires?"

Clive's morning routine was supposed to encompass personal calls to the local police and fire stations, the council offices, parish church and the waterworks to ascertain what, if anything, had occurred during the previous 24 hours that may be of interest to readers. In truth, Clive was a late riser and a fan of the 'phone. He felt that a quick ring round would suffice although his mileage claims suggested a daily average that would have top rally drivers purring in admiration.

"Well, there were no fires…."

"So that's one par. Anything else? Crimes?"

"Er…a bit of vandalism."

"Go on."

"Graffiti on a bus shelter."

"What did it say?"

"Bollocks to Tring"

"Is that it?"

"Just about."

"Well, a good and productive morning's work, Clive"

"Cheers." His accompanying snort of laughter did not go down well with Chrissy.

"If I were you," she said icily, "I'd try and conjure up something a little more substantial else you know who'll do his nut."

Clive reluctantly reached for his notebook and started searching through the scribble for something comprehensible that could stand converting into what might pass as a story. His efforts were interrupted by a cigar-smoking Harry Symonds, who was heading purposefully towards him.

"Hi, Boss. Coffee?"

"Never mind about coffee…what about some copy?"

"Hey, Boss, I like it."

"Whether you 'like it' is of no concern to me, Clive. Have you done any stories yet?"

"Nearly finished one, Boss."

"Well hurry up…I want to get something over to Hemel on the bus."

The Gazette had an informal arrangement for copy delivery with the drivers of the 301C. Janet or one of the reporters would wait at the Berkhamsted town centre bus stop with a package of copy, adverts and miscellaneous paperwork which would be placed in the driver's glove compartment and handed over to a waiting staffer at the Hemel Hempstead bus station.

Mr. Symonds then turned his gaze on me. "Has Chrissy given you something to do?"

I reddened. "Um, yes. I'm, er working on it at the moment." I offered up a quick prayer that he would not ask to see my public toilets repainting effort.

"Alright. Well done. Let me have a look at it when you've finished." With that he marched backed to his office leaving a cloud of blue cigar smoke in his wake.

Chrissy, who had not even glanced in our direction during the exchange, continued to hammer furiously at her typewriter as Janet dealt with a customer at the front desk who wanted to place an ad in the for sale column.

"What should I do?" I whispered desperately.

"Tell you what," she responded. "I've done a few stories from the Rural Council minutes. You have a look at the reports and my stories, see how I've done them, and have a crack at one or two yourself. But don't just copy what I've written. See if you can come up with any fresh angles."

"Thanks, Chrissy." I took the papers and her copy. "By the way, what did you do with my public toilets repainting story?"

She pursed her lips and slowly lowered her eyes to the bin next to her desk and then looked back to her typewriter and resumed her qwerty pounding.

I kept quiet. I probably didn't realise it at the time, but I had just passed my first test in journalism.

Chapter 6

That night saw me sitting alongside Chrissy in the chamber of Berkhamsted Urban District Council with the agenda for the finance and general purposes committee in front of me. The items on the agenda were accompanied by recommendations for approval, rejection or deferral. The information seemed a bit thin.

As the meeting got under way, the apologies for absence were noted, minutes of last meeting approved and matters arising dealt with in the space of a minute or two. This is alright, I thought, I'll be away inside 20 minutes at this rate…be able to get back to see some world cup highlights. England had opened their campaign with a goalless draw against Uruguay. Jimmy Greaves hadn't been able to score which was a bit of a worry….but, he's got to come good…I mean his scoring record in league games has been fantastic. And Bobby Charlton just looks different class...

"Item 4 …grass cutting cycle at cemetery".

The voice of the committee chairman interrupted my thought processes. I'll have to defer consideration of the England team selection until later.

"Mr Chairman, I cannot believe that estimate in paragraph three can be accurate. I'm sure that figure can't be right. It's a big increase on what we've had to pay in the past…"

Chrissy was scribbling away taking notes whilst I desperately searched for paragraph three to see what the councillor was talking about. Never mind paragraph three, I couldn't detect paragraphs one or two. What was going on?

"Where's these paragraphs?" I whispered to Chrissy.

"Shut up and concentrate on taking notes; I'll explain later."

"Well, Councillor Jones, that's the figure we have to deal with. If you look at paragraph seven, you'll see why there has been such an increase."

Paragraph seven. *Paragraph seven*! What is happening here? How can you take notes about invisible paragraphs for Christ's sake?

And so it went on. Item after item was commented on by the assembled 22 councillors. Cryptic comments were made and even one 'declaration of interest'. *Declaration of interest!* How can anybody be interested in this twaddle?

After a couple of hours the Chairman mercifully brought proceedings to a halt with a reminder of the date for the next meeting. I sat staring at the pile of notes I had made in pidgin Pitman's, wondering how the hell I was going to be able to produce any copy. Chrissy had buttonholed the council treasurer who sat down with her and clarified some of the figures and decisions.
"Is this your first meeting?"

I looked up from my notes into the face of the chairman.

"Yes. I've just started on the Gazette."

"How did you find it?"

"Em, fine" I lied.

"Good. I'll look forward to seeing the write-up. Well, goodnight."

"Yes, er goodnight."

"Come on Paul, let's pop down to The Swan. I'm gasping."

I suddenly felt better and trotted alongside Chrissy as she led the way out of the council offices and into the still warm evening air.

Over a pint and a g and t in the saloon bar, we discussed what had happened at the meeting.

"How are we supposed to write stories about what was going on when we don't have the reports that the councillors are talking about? It's impossible."

"No it isn't, darling. You'll get used to it once you've attended a few meetings. We get the minutes of the meetings and after a while you get to know what they're talking about. The most important part of the meeting is picking the brains of the officers afterwards. You can make up most of the councillors' quotes."

"Make up quotes! But that's…that's, well that's…er wrong. Isn't it?"

"Oooh no darling. On the contrary. Most of the councillors can't string two words together and are only too grateful for us making them appear half ways intelligent. In any case, they'll not remember what they said."

"But supposing they claim that they've been misquoted?"

"We offer to show them our notes of the meeting."

"Yes, but you just admitted you made up the quotes."

She sighed in that irritating way that mothers and teachers do when one of their charges has asked a stupid question. "If, and it's a big if, they actually turn up and demand to see my notes, I show them. And what will they see?

"I don't understand."

"Well, darling, all they'll see is my scribbled shorthand which'll mean absolutely bugger-all to them. Anyway, it hasn't happened yet. Another pint?"

My second lesson in journalism had been learnt.

Chapter 7

One of my stories did make it on to the front page of the first Gazette - edition, June 10 - that I had been working on.

I gazed at it with pride.

Under the 14pt times bold u&l heading **Cesspool Trouble** the single column piece read:

Because Berkhamsted Rural Council's two cesspool emptying machines cannot cope with the number of requests for emptying, the Council are to buy a third machine.

There is a six month delivery time for the vehicle.

My first couple of weeks were spent doing the dogsbody work of delivering packages to the 301C, getting Harry Symonds' daily supply of Castellas and gin, knocking out short stories from council reports, fillers (single paragraphs of copy usually recording a petty crime, chimney fire or minor road accident, that were invaluable for sticking under stories to fill a column) and doing the weddings. The weddings were easy; the Gazette had a form with various sections that the bride and groom and their familes could complete and return, together with a photo, to our office. The completed form had all the necessary information that was needed for the reports, such as wedding and reception venues, names of bride and groom, best man, bridesmaids and matron of honour, respective parents, style of dress and going-away outfits and honeymoon destination. The trick was to try and vary the intros so that the reports did not appear too formulaic. I was also expected to come up with headlines for the reports. These usually consisted of something like "EDWARDIAN-STYLE DRESS FOR LOCAL BRIDE" or "TO LIVE IN NORTHCHURCH". Unnervingly perhaps, such headlines were usually approved without demur and

I started to get over confident. Fortunately Chrissy managed to blue pencil my suggested title over a wedding of a nurse and patient which proclaimed "ROMANCE STARTED IN HOSPITAL BED".

Chrissy and I continued to attend the evening meetings of the urban district council and its committees, and the morning sessions of the rural district council whose membership included the local squire Sir Edward Brown. Sir Edward was in his late seventies and was an arch-attender. Unfortunately his physical presence was not matched by a mental presence. I found it difficult not to laugh as the old buffer snoozed his way through item after item, snoring gently and occasionally mumbling "jolly good – approved". His fellow members tolerated his approach to local democracy and rarely disturbed him except to wake him in time for lunch.

I have to say that I was pretty content with life…I could accurately call myself a reporter and England had reached the semi-final of the world cup. I had been desperate to go to the game against Portugal and Chrissy's dad had pulled in a couple of favours to get me a ticket.

I had managed to buy a second hand Underwood typewriter for £2.10s from a contact of Chrissy's at the Hemel Hempstead office where staff worked on the small group's main paper – the Hemel Hempstead Gazette. On the day I was due to collect the machine Harry Symonds had suggested that he accompany me. For 'accompany' read 'give a lift home'.

The Hemel Gazette office, situated opposite the town hall, at Warwick House, 39 Marlowes was located in a fine three-storey Georgian town house in which resided the chief editor, reporters, advertising staff, photographers and the managing director, Thomas Robinson. The group of papers, Hertfordshire Newspapers

Ltd., which also included the Tring and District News, was a family-owned concern.

As I drew up, Harry Symonds who had been sleeping off his lunchtime excesses in the passenger seat announced that he would be getting out to discuss 'important mattersh with Ronnie'. By now, I realised that for Harry Symonds, extrication from the front passenger seat of a Ford Anglia was a complicated and time-consuming exercise. Being around 16 stone and six foot, Harry was anything but an agile or swift mover. I opened the passenger door, took his brief case and then started to pull on his left arm. Simultaneously he attempted to swing his left leg out of the car only for it to jam in the foot well.

"Jushhaminnit….leg…shrapnel….Dusseldorf….'43."

I let go of his arm and started to try and free the wedged leg. He flopped back like a puppet whose strings had been cut.

"You'll have to lean across to the driver's side so I can lift the leg out of the car, Mr Symonds."

"Anything you shay dear boy."

As he leaned sideways I was able to pull the leg free and place his size twelve foot on to the kerb. I then resumed the arm pulling routine and slowly but surely, the bulk that was the editor of the Berkhamsted Gazette emerged into the Hemel Hempstead sunshine. At this point I was convinced I could hear a noise that sounded like people cheering but was unable to ascertain its origin.

"Quick, come and have a look at this." Wendy Jobson, chief Hemel reporter called colleagues to the window of editor Ronnie Dean's office which overlooked Marlowes. "It's Symonds from Berko and he's pissed as a newt."

The next 90 seconds were punctuated with gales of laughter and applause as each stage of the Berkhamsted editor car extraction project was completed.

"Oh Gawd, not Symonds. I'm off. Alright you lot. Show's over. Back to work." Ronnie Dean ushered the giggling staffers from his office, reached for his jacket and lit the day's thirtieth Embassy. Ronnie, a mid-forties tall avuncular presence, had been a local journalist since leaving school. He had risen through the ranks and had a very direct approach to what went in the paper: "Loads of names, court cases, plenty of funerals and weddings." Stories on the fringes of the distribution area were treated with disdain no matter how good. Even a multiple pile-up on the nearby M1 would only get a passing mention unless there was an " 'emel person" involved. And his strictures to the errant reporters producing unacceptable copy usually involved the criticism that "it don't flow Flossie/Nimrod/boy/honkytonk - the latter soubriquet reserved for any male reporter who might turn up wearing a pastel shirt. Puzzled hacks pressing for further clarification would be told "too many wibble-wobbles/queer things". Strangely the advice worked in that once the offending scribe had re-read his or her copy, the mistakes were all too apparent

"Wend… I'm off down 'The Sip and Swaller' (The Whip and Collar ale house which was situated opposite the Roses Lime juice depot next to the Grand Union Canal). I don't want to have to talk to the old fool. Get rid of him will you, dear?"

"What do I tell him, Ronnie?"

"Oh, make something up Wend….you know, like one of yer quotes." He chuckled as he left for the rear exit of the building.

Wendy returned to the main reporters' room. Eight scruffy Formica tables, with their accompanying typewriters, and assorted filing cabinets cluttered the area. Wendy had been with the Gazette for nearly 20 years and was well respected by the collection of mainly youngish reporters. The one middle-aged hack was Norman Peterson, a fine wordsmith when he could be bothered, whose reputation for diligent searching for the perfect pub far exceeded that of his journalistic work ethic.

The shoulder to cry on – an essential for any office where egos are constantly pricked by reality – was Rita Fielding, the chief sub whose placid journey through life was a constant reassurance to her fellow hacks. It was Rita who was usually deputed to deal with outraged misquotees, and vengeful villains who resented publicity given by the Gazette to their magistrates' courts appearances.

Crime reporting was the speciality of Suzie Harrison whose ability to get inside information from police sources had more to do with her flirting with the local nick's desk sergeant than journalistic sleuthing.

Suzie's immediate desk neighbour was Jane Attwood. She was the baby of the office who, like me, was less reporter and more gopher in her first few weeks. The morning cry from Ronnie as he rolled in was ' Oi, Flossie, get me a cuppa, well larruped and pop down the shop for twenty Embassy and a box of strikers'. She had originally wondered why her boss had not simply stopped his car outside the shop and purchased aforementioned smoking material himself until it dawned on her that such an operation would have involved getting out of his vehicle, an act Ronnie considered only necessary after every possible bit of driveable tarmac had been consumed en route to the office. As with, perversely, every female trainee reporter before her, Jane was the paper's mythical 'Uncle George', the avuncular font of wisdom for the Gazette's 'Children's Corner' readership. It was she who set the competitions, bought prizes, typed up birth dates of Corner members and wrote little homilies about generally being good to small animals and old ladies.

Opposite Jane sat another recent recruit, Melvin Thompson. Despite his junior status Melvin, who was convinced of his likeness to Steve McQueen, felt he was the paper's principal asset. A penchant for trying to pen pieces using formats gleaned from The Melody Maker and New Musical Express usually brought him into conflict with Wendy after she had re-written his copy to comply with the Gazette's style.

Brian Dickson was the paper's resident boffin; a studious, quiet and ultra shy young man whose decision to go into journalism had shocked his parents and school who assumed his future lay in academia. Historical facts, both local and national, mathematical problems and geographical references were always checked with Brian before being committed to print.

Brian's quiet modest intelligent presence was in stark contrast to that of Roger Parsons whose lack of nous was camouflaged by an astonishing but wholly unjustifiable self-confidence. It was Roger who was usually responsible for the paper's legendary howlers that were fondly recalled for decades to come. When covering a story of a surgeon's 'miraculous' work in bringing a patient out of a coma Roger posed the following question: "And how long was it before the patient was reincarnated?". But his all-time greatest contribution to howler folklore was the query: "Are you married?" History hasn't recorded the Roman Catholic's priest's reply.

A battered door led to an adjoining room frequented by sports reporters Keith Cheeseborough and Phil Benning. Phil lived for football. An Arsenal fan, Phil could name every Gunners team that had won the league or FA Cup since the inception of the competitions. His enthusiasm for local soccer was nearly as passionate as his interest in The Gunners and many's the time a local player's profile would be lifted by being likened by Phil to an Arsenal star. As Phil was addicted to soccer, Keith's loves were cricket and, in particular, Surrey CCC, and horse racing. Although just 20, Keith eschewed all that mid-1960s fashion had to offer and opted for the type of sober apparel that had the ageing tailors at the Hemel branch of Dunne's smiling with joy. And as the lengthening hair and bushy sideburns of the era became de rigueur for the male staff, Keith stuck doggedly to the Charles Buchan short back and sides of his dad's generation.

Along the corridor towards the rear of the building was Tommy's office. Thomas Robinson, the managing director came into the office every day although, in truth, his appearance was more a matter of form than necessity. His family had owned the company for many years and he had drifted into the position following the death of his father. Tommy was not a journalist and would not know a good story if it bit him in the buttocks. His accountancy training background meant that the only thing he read were the quarterly sales figures for circulation and advertising. His one weekly contribution was to devise the paper's 'silly ad', a mysteriously popular weekly spoof advertisement that was inserted in the columns of the classifieds that filled the centre pages. Gems such as: "Wanted. Reliable man or woman to budgie-sit; cuttlefish supplied, must be good conversationalist. Apply Mr Perch, 10 Millet Lane, Berkhamsted" or "Bicycle bells wanted by Tring collector."

The June 24th 1966 effort was a gem. Under the column heading 'Medical' was the following: "HAVE you a troublesome cough? Then you need Plastikoffdrops! One Plastikoffdrop, because it does not wear out, will suffice for the whole family for years, provided it is not trodden on or dropped in the fire; after using, just dip in a jar of Plastikoffdrop syrup and it is ready for immediate use; from your chemist or stores, Plastikoffdrop, complete with jar of syrup, 4s 6d each."

The following week's paper recorded the winning silly ad spotter as Mrs I W Grabarczyk of 4 Hillmay Drive, Hemel Hempstead who received two guineas for her observational skills. Mrs I M Clarke of 35 Great Road, Hemel Hempstead had to be satisfied with second place and a fifteen shilling postal order, whilst the doubtless disappointed third-placed Miss V Henry of 20 Pancake Lane, Leverstock Green would find herself just 10s 6d richer. Possibly slightly bemused were the directors of W H Smith, with a ten shillings award thanks to the stationer's Marlowes, Hemel Hempstead branch having sold the paper to the aforementioned Mrs Grabarczyk.

Downstairs from Tommy's office lived the advertising and administration staff, and in the basement - "The Hole" – in which was situated the dark room where photographers Eric, Simon and Billy printed and developed the pictures which were converted to etched Graphalloy plates on the recently purchased American made Photolathe, one of only a few UK local newspapers to acquire such a machine.

The Photolathe looked similar to a conventional workshop lathe and had two 9inch diameter cylinders.

On the left hand cylinder, printed photos were secured face up under a transferring celluloid sheet.

On the right hand cylinder, two rows of teeth held a thin (1.5mm) strip of flexible metal - Graphalloy (a combination of graphite and metal) - measuring about two foot long by 18 inches wide.

The lathe had an electromagnetic device which contained a stylus. As the cylinders simultaneously rotated, a photocell detector on a thread drive within the lathe traversed the left hand cylinder scanning the pictures and directed the stylus to etch the metal sheet to varying depths to trace the white and black elements of the photos.

The procedure lasted about 45 minutes. On average about 10 pictures could be produced in each spin cycle.

At the end of the process, the picture images would be cut from the strip by guillotine to fit the broadsheet Gazette one and seven eighths inch column widths-- from single to full-page eight-column --and depths of up to 20 inches. The cut Graphalloy pieces were taken to the printing works at the bottom of Warners End Road at its junction with the Leighton Buzzard road where they were affixed to appropriately sized wooden blocks. These were then laid into a chase alongside the lead type of the text and headlines in readiness for printing.

Eric Taylor, the chief photographer, rode a Triumph Matchless 500cc and would usually appear for a job in soaking black leathers, with his shock of black crinkly hair standing bolt upright. Eric, notionally single but with a complicated love life involving two fiancées, was a keen guitarist and a familiar face at pub-based folk clubs whose clientele preferred Martin Carthy and Dave Swarbrick to the Beatles.

Number two in the snappers' pecking order was Simon Teasdale whose preferred mode of transport was the VW Beetle from which he would acknowledge fellow VW drivers with a friendly salute.

The trainee, Billy Baxendale who had recently joined the Gazette, proudly sported mod garb and rode a Lambretta which bore at least six headlights and a fox tail on an aerial attached to the seat.

Chapter 8

As I walked behind Harry Symonds towards the Gazette front entrance I glanced up at the window from which I thought I had heard laugher but could see nothing.

"Now dear boy, I jush going to shee Mr Dean. You jush shtay downshtairs….I don't want you mixshing with the shtaff….there'sh a lot you don't know."

'*There's a lot you don't know?*' What the hell is he on about. Of course there's a lot I don't know; I've never been here before.

As we walked into the dingy foyer at the foot of the stairs, Wendy greeted us.

"Oh hi, Harry. What brings you over?"

Harry. *Harry*! She called him Harry – to his face! What a nerve. She'd better look out. If there's one thing I did know, it was that Harry Symonds had a high degree of self regard and was not a person to be taken lightly. He was the Editor of the Berkhamsted Gazette and, as the holder of such a lofty position, an above average level of deference from reporters of our sister paper must surely be required. I winced in anticipation of a barrage of outrage.

"Hello Wendy sweetie. Can I shay how lovely you're looking today."

I was still between the states of bewilderment and confusion when Wendy looked past him in my direction and grinned.

"You can. And who's this you have with you?"

"Oh thish ish…thish ish…er Peter…"

"Paul…"

"Er….yesh…er Paul…um Paul…"

"Barnes."

"Hi Paul. I'm Wendy Jobson. So you're the latest hack to join our crusade to educate and inform. Welcome to HQ. Are you coming up to see the folks?"

"Good idea, dear boy. You go off and shee them whilsht I shee Mishter Dean."

"Sorry, Harry. Ronnie's had to go off to an important meeting. He won't be back until tomorrow. He asked me to take a message. What do you want me to tell him?"

"Hessh bloody elushi…elush…er difficult to catch. He never sheems to be here when I want to shee him. I won't leave a meshidge. I'll jush pop in and shee Tommy."

Harry stumbled towards the stairs and leaned against the banister rail. Wendy and I gazed at him as he pulled his frame up the steps to the first floor corridor.

"Well Paul, how about coming up and meeting the slaves. I think they know you're in the building."

"Do they? How?"

"They were witnessing your heroic Symonds extraction manoeuvre after you parked up."

"Oh, was it you lot that were laughing?"

"Oh, there might have been the odd titter. Never mind, come along."

The next few minutes were lost amid a welter of welcoming banter and references to Harry Symonds's love of gin. As I gazed at the sea of faces my eyes settled on Jane a little too long perhaps as she reddened slightly and pretended to read some copy in her typewriter. She had longish fair hair and wore a mini-skirt that did a lot for her legs and much to crank up my usual thought processes on meeting a fanciable girl. Hmmm…wonder if she's got a bloke….bird like that'll probably have someone on the go…still might be worth a crack…

Wendy broke into my daydream. "Paul, when you've finished gawping at our Jane, I'll take you down the hole to meet the photographers."

"Um, er, yes. Great. Um, see you all again. Cheers."

The hole was aptly named. With a strong whiff of chemicals, the tiny converted cellar had no natural light and was barely big enough for one person to occupy let alone the three snappers the Gazette employed.

The dark room door at the foot of the narrow staircase was adorned with cartoon skull and crossbones and bore the legend 'knock before entering – or die'. Wendy rapped loudly on the door only to be greeted with a shout of "piss off; we're busy…"

"Don't be a berk, Eric. Open up. I've got a visitor."

Wendy turned to me, smiling. "Don't be put off by his uncouth demeanour; he's really a sweetie. But, there is a very good reason for not barging straight in. The merest glimmer of light entering the dark room during processing could totally bugger up half a dozen photo jobs."

The door opened and Eric ushered us in. "Hi Wend…sorry … haven't even got time for a quickie, ha ha….who's this?"

Ignoring Eric's less than romantic sexual reference, Wendy introduced me. "This is Paul, Paul Barnes. He's just started over at Berko."

"Poor sod," said Eric. "Still, Chrissy'll see you ok. Have you given her one yet?"

"Er, no." I felt my face redden. While I hadn't given… I mean, had not had any sexual encounter with Chrissy, I had thought about it.

" Er…how do you do. Er, what's it like here?"

Eric scoffed loudly. "Well, Paul, where do I start? I spend four hours a day stuck down in this hole, breathing in fumes in semi-darkness, printing and developing pictures of fat birds in parachute wedding dresses and the bleedin' mayor planting yet another bleedin' tree, and old trouts doing 'good works' for even older trouts. And that's the better part of the job. At least I'm dry. The rest of my time is spent out, usually in the pissing rain, trying to get some bolshie kid to smile and hold up his trophy for winning the bleedin' egg and bleedin' spoon race at the Potten End bleedin' fete…."

Wendy cut in. "Eric's always a bit testy at this time of the day. Don't worry, sweetie, they'll be open shortly. Where are the other two herberts, Eric?"

"Billy's at some pile-up on the A41 and Simon's doing a school sports day. Anyway, nice meeting you Paul. And, remember, if you want me to do a photo job for you, you've only to ask….!"

I made a mental note to request the photographic services of Simon or Billy when the need arose.

Chapter 9

The same issue that announced the benefits of the Plastikoffdrop epitomised the Gazette's approach to local events during Harry's tenure of the Berkhamsted office. He was particularly keen on supporting/sucking-up to the town's well-heeled glitterati. And Founder's Day, the annual bun-fight of Berkhamsted School – then an all-male establishment – was just such an occasion. To say the paper covered the event is akin to recording that the BBC gives the odd mention to the US presidential election. What made the 1966 event extra-special for Harry was the attendance of Miss B W Russell MA, Head of Berkhamsted Girls School. There they were: the two leaders of public school academic excellence, together in a glorious tableau of educational privilege, Miss R and Mr B H Garnons-Williams (we never published his first name, oh dear me, no) Head of Berkhamsted School.

Harry was in semi-pickled heaven, sitting on the stage in the quadrangle amongst the governors and guests, waving and grinning at people he believed he recognised in the audience. I took notes and compiled information for the page and a half spread of tightly packed text and photos. The following headlines appeared on page two:

 FOUNDERS DAY HAD ALL THE HIGHLIGHTS – in Times Roman caps over *It Was an Occasion When Two "Heads" Get Together* in 36 point Times Roman italics (Harry's personal favourite headline font) over (more Times Roman caps) A "RED ROSE" DAY WHICH WAS UNIQUE which adjoined a four column picture of the two heads and governors under yet another headline - The Governors – And a Very Special Guest – Arrive With Red Rose for Founders Day.

Wow, I thought, if this doesn't shift a few copies, I don't know what will.

Chapter 10

As my first few weeks of local hackery developed without too many gaffes another important event was taking place: England was staging the World Cup and, well, it looked as if Alf Ramsey's statement that we would win the competition was not just an idle headline-grabber. The team had safely navigated its way through the group stages with wins against France and Mexico and a draw against Uruguay to finish top with five points. Truth be told they had not looked very convincing and Greavesie had failed to score. How could he not score? I mean, surely he's going to stick one in eventually. And then came news that Ramsey had dropped him for the quarter-final match against Argentina. Drop Greaves…..how could he? The man's gone bonkers. Our most important game – ever – and he's gambling on Geoff Hurst of West Ham, virtually untried, to take over up front. Oh, no. What can he be thinking of? Alright, yes, Hurst did score and we won one-nil, but that was due in large part to Argentina playing for nearly an hour with ten men after their captain Antonio Rattin was sent off. Ramsey will see sense for the semi-final and restore Greaves to his rightful position, won't he?

Oh no, he hasn't. He's sticking with Hurst.

And I'm going to the match.

I'd been going on in the office about the world cup, bleating about Ramsey's nonsensical team selection when Chrissy interjected.

"Are you going to the match?"

"No…..I'd never get a ticket."

"I might be able to get you a ticket."

"Whaaat.….could you?"

"Yes. One of Dad's mates looks after the catering at Wembley. He's been able to get tickets and offered one to Dad, but he can't go. I'm sure he'll be able to get it for you."

"Oh, that would be bleedin' great. Oh, thanks, thank you very much…."

"Well, you can start showing your gratitude by getting me a coffee."

"I'll get you your coffee every day for a year if you can get me the ticket."

As luck would have it, the ticket was passed to Chrissy's dad the following day. And on that warm late July evening the ticket was tucked safely in my pocket as I made my way towards Wembley on the Metropolitan line. As the train rumbled south I started to have gnawing doubts about what lay ahead. We're playing Portugal, who've beaten Brazil let's not forget, and Eusebio, the tournament's top scorer is on fire. We haven't conceded a goal in the competition and I'm going to the game where we're going to get slaughtered thanks to Ramsey's cock-eyed thinking.

What a genius that Alf Ramsey is. Two – one. Bobby Charlton gets a goal in both halves. Eusebio pulls one back from a penalty with eight minutes to go creating some buttock-clenching, religion-discovering, nail-biting, swearing moments to endure before Monsieur Schwinte mercifully blows the full-time whistle. Cue delirious applause and hugging of complete strangers in that moment of joyous nationalism. A few yards away, a group of Portugese supporters console each other and I feel a surge of guilt, which lasts for nearly five seconds.

"Hmm. Might write a few pars about the game for the Gazette….Wonder if I can find a Berko connection?…..Wouldn't it be great if Geoff Hurst's mum lived in the area…"

That euphoric Wednesday night merely served to intensify my hopes for a final victory against West Germany who'd also got to the last stage with a two – one victory, over the USSR. Regrettably, Chrissy's dad was unable to repeat the ticket miracle and I watched the game at home, alone, getting progressively more rat-arsed and emotional as the extra time drama drew to a conclusion with the Kenneth Wolstenholme words: "Some people are on the pitch – they think it's all over (Hurst scores his third, and England's fourth, past a static and bewildered Tilkowski); it is now."

Chapter 11

The combination of England winning and, for me, an inordinate amount of alcohol (four pints) contributed to a euphoria which emboldened me to do something special: I'd ring Jane and ask her out; she'd bound to be interested….

Ahh…..problem…..don't have her number. Wait a minute, what about Directory Enquiries? They'll have her number. I managed to dial 192 without too much trouble.

"Er hello…erm, 'ave you….'ave you got the number of Attwood?"

"Do you have the full address and initial, caller?"

Shit. I don't know where she lives. And it wouldn't be her initial, she probably lives at home with her folks, so it'll be her dad or mum's initial.

"Er…I only know tha ish Hemel Hempshtead. I don't know the in..the in..inisshuull…."

"Hold on (pause)…Hello caller, there are six Attwoods in the directory for the Hemel Hempstead."

"Can I have them all pleash?"

"All the numbers?"

"If you'd be sho kind."

"Hemel Hempstead 2613, Hemel Hempstead 4008, Hem….are you still there caller?"

I'd dropped the 'phone and was looking for a piece of paper and a pen. Found a pen. Couldn't see any paper. I staggered to the outside toilet and ripped some sheets from the toilet roll.

"Shorry 'bout that. Had to get a peesh of paper. What are the numbersh? Er hello….hello….ahggh bollocksh….sheeshungup."

I started to re-dial directory enquiries, when it hit me. It was the unmistakeable jolt of slightly painful fuzziness that rockets from the toes to the head via the eyes: I was on the one-way ticket to chucking up with just the slightest pause at the whirly pits siding. Even at 21, I knew there was no turning back, so out into the back garden past a smirking brother for the inevitable alarming, but unstoppable shouting and outpouring. Was winning the world cup worth this distress? What a silly question.

Later that evening as the pounding in my head began to fade I reflected that the silver lining to my vomit-coloured cloud was the failure to make contact with Jane in such a state.

I'll call her tomorrow.

I didn't.

Chapter 12

When I started on the Gazette, I was told that I would be indentured. Avoiding a juvenile quip about not wanting my teeth straightened I enquired as to what 'being indentured' meant.

"It's what might be described in industry as an apprenticeship," said Harry. "If after your probationary period we think you're worth taking on, we'll get you signed up with your articles."

"Er….articles?"

"Yes, your articles of apprenticeship."

"Oh, er….right, those articles. Well, thank you."

I hadn't got a clue what articles he meant, Did I have to write some for the paper? Were they objects? Private parts? I'll ask Chrissy later.

"Oh, it's just a poncey word meaning period of training," said Chrissy. "Don't worry…it just means you'll be stuck here for three years. You'll get called to sign up at Hemel."

And, sure enough, on September 15, 1966 I was summoned to appear at Tommy's office. What I didn't realise, because we had never met, was that Tommy had a lisp.

A small man in a pin stripe suit with a waistcoat, Tommy did not exactly fit the picture of a cigar chewing hard-nosed newspaper proprietor. Peering over his tiny glasses he beckoned me to sit down.

"Ah, Mithter Barnth, I'm pleathed to say that we would like to invite you to thign your arthicles of apprenthiceship."

Arthicles of apprenthiship? What the hell is he on about?

He passed over the form.

"Oh, my articles of apprenticeship."

"Yeth, Mithter Barnth. Thath what I thaid. Read it through, and if you acthept the terms pleathe thign it."

I started to read the form which seemed to have been concocted from wording in the Magna Carta. Part of it went as follows: 'Mr Paul Barnes……doth put himself apprenticed to Messrs. Hertfordshire Newspapers Limited of Warwick House, 39, Marlowes, Hemel Hempstead in the same County, hereinafter called the Master….to learn the art of Journalism and with them after the manner of an apprentice serve from the fifteenth day of September one thousand nine hundred and sixty six to 20th December, 1969 thence next ensuing during which term the said apprentice shall faithfully serve his master keep his secrets and do his lawful commands, he shall do no damage to or waste or make away with his master's property or materials but shall warn his master if he shall see others do likewise. He shall not gamble nor frequent taverns but shall be of good behaviour, he shall not absent himself from his master's service and in all things he shall behave himself towards his master during the said term.'

Blimey…no drinking or gambling! That's the pools and the pub gone for a Burton. And what's that about secrets? What secrets? Is Tommy having it away with one of the staff? Does he wear women's clothing?

As for the next clause….well, needless to say it was a bargain most unlikely to be entirely honoured: 'The parent hereby covenants with the principal to find and provide the apprentice with board and lodgings and suitable clothing and all other necessaries during the term of apprenticeship and the principals hereby agree to pay the said apprentice as per the agreed scale.'

Well I didn't get board, lodging or clothing, but I did get the agreed scale - £11 4s 10p per week. (Less, incidentally, than I had been previously earning as a junior executive at TAM) Oh, yes. I drive a hard bargain, me.

"Er, um…that theems…er seems fine Mr Robinson….I'll just sign then?"

I signed and Tommy then added his signature.

"And, you'll need to get it signed by your parent and witnessed by someone else who knows you," he said.

"Ah, right, um…thank you very much."

Tommy stood up and shook my hand. "We hope that you'll enjoy your work here, Mr Barnth."

I felt great. I was now, officially, a reporter – albeit an apprentice. I wandered into the main reporters' office to share my good news. In truth, I was hoping that Jane would be there. She wasn't. The room was empty. Well, it was gone four.

Later that day I showed the form to Mum who was beaming as she signed.

"Who shall I get to witness? Will Gran do?"

"Of course. But make sure her bloody hearing aid's on," said Mum.

As I got to her room the radio was blaring so I knew I had a battle on my hands.

Puffing on a Woodbine, she put down the Daily Mirror and smiled at me.

"Hello, dear."

"Hello, Gran…..I need you to witness my indentures," I shouted.

"What's that dear?"

"I need you to – have you got your hearing aid turned on?"

"Ay? What's that?"

"HAVE YOU GOT YOUR HEARING AID TURNED ON?"

"Hold on a minute dear….I'll just turn my hearing aid on."

This was a familiar conversation in the Barnes household. Our gran had come to live with us when we moved to Highfield Road, Bushey in Hertfordshire from our semi-detached bungalow in nearby Carpenders Park. She was as deaf as a post and it used to drive Mum potty that she wouldn't keep her hearing aid on. But for brother John and I, her deafness was a delight. Many's the idle afternoon we'd while away talking bollocks to Gran knowing that she couldn't hear. But when we wanted her to hear, a well-experienced routine would be enacted: we'd bellow, she'd respond; we'd bellow, she'd ask what we were saying; we'd bellow and eventually she would start fumbling around the cardigan that covered her ample bosom to find the old NHS hearing aid. There would then follow some strange whistling noises as the aid chugged into life to make communication a possibility. As the whistling ceased and the earplug pressed into place, the conversation could begin.

I hovered over her as she completed the manoeuvres.

"I need you to witness my indentures."

"What are they, dear?"

"It's a form which I need to get signed by people who know me to say that I agree to being an apprentice reporter."

"You're going to be a porter, dear ? Like your granddad? That's nice."

"No, Gran. A REporter….you know, like a journalist…..somebody who writes for the paper."

"You're going to write to the paper, dear? What about? Is it about the dog muck on the pavements?"

"No, Gran. I'm going to be a….yes, ok, a porter. Just sign here will you."

"Alright, dear."

She scrawled her name on the dotted line next to 'in the presence of'.

"There you are, dear. Ooh a porter, eh. What station?"

"Berkhamsted."

"Birkenhead?"

"Yes, Gran."

"That's nice, dear."

Chapter 13

One of the first rules of journalism is to engage the reader's interest in a story in the first few lines; the opening paragraph has to give people a pretty good idea of what the piece is about.

The following is the opening par, across three columns in italics, from the front page lead story of issue of September 23, 1966:
"After all these years of almost dying hopes, it is very pleasing to see this item on the agenda today," commented County Councillor S. H. Smith at the meeting of Hertfordshire Fire Brigade Committee on Friday.

"Well that should get the readers reaching for the smelling salts," said Chrissy. "That's Harry all over; he can't write to save his life. If you produce copy like that Paul, I'll have your guts for garters."

The story went on, across two columns: He was referring to a recommendation that approval be given to the purchase of the site known as Matthews Yard, Castle Street, Berkhamsted, for the erection of a Fire and Ambulance Station.

"If he wrote better, he wouldn't have to shove all those bloody headlines over the story….look at it."

She had a point. There were three separate headlines before the opening par. A 14 point strap head across three and a half columns: "THIS WILL PUT A STOP TO OBSOLETE CONDITIONS" – was followed by a 36 point Times Roman italic headline across six and four columns:
S.H. Smith: "Give Them The Place From
Which To Fight Fires!"

And to complete the set, across three and three came, in 24 pt bold caps:

HE CHAMPIONS A NEW SITE FOR FIRE BRIGADE AND AMBULANCE

"He might just as well not bothered with writing any copy if he's going to put that lot on top of the page," she said.

Blimey, I thought, he's the Editor. Surely he knows how to write a story. I had read it before Chrissy's outburst and thought nothing of the way it was written.

Perhaps there's more to this reporting game than I first imagined. Fortunately fate in the shapely guise of Jane Attwood intervened.

Chapter 14

Jane Attwood and a couple of the other Hemel reporters had discovered, through the UK Press Gazette, that the National Council for the Training of Journalists was advertising its courses for indentured reporters. A number of colleges of further education throughout the UK staged day release or block release courses for aspiring hacks. The courses included English, local government, law, shorthand, practical journalism and current affairs and led to a final exam and a Proficiency certificate. At that time, nobody on the Gazette had ever taken part in such courses; training, such as it was, took place 'on the job'. Tommy Robinson was not keen on his staff being away from the office for such purposes and Jane and her colleagues had fought a tough battle to get him to change his mind.

It was Chrissy who took the call. "Oh, hi Jane. How's things?"

Jane….Jane Attwood? I stopped typing the fifth wedding report of the day. I strained to listen to the conversation. Eventually, Chrissy glanced over to me.

"I don't know whether he can come to the 'phone," she said grinning at me. "Oh, no, here he is."

I stumbled out of my chair and grabbed the 'phone.

"…'er, um, hello Jane. What? Training course. Oh, I don't know." My heart sank. This was turning out to be a double disappointment. Not only was Jane not ringing to invite me to some party or other she was asking whether I wanted my name added to those who wanted to go on an NCTJ course. I thought my days of training courses and exams were over and I really didn't want to do it.

"I'm going on one," she said.

"Me too."

"Great, I'll tell Ronnie and he can square it with Tommy for you to go. Is Clive there?"

"No. But I'll ask him whether he's interested or not when he returns."

"Ok. 'Bye."

"Goodbye, Jane……er…um see you."

"No guessing why you agreed to go on one of those courses," ventured Chrissy.

"I think I should learn more about my craft."

"My craft, bollocks. You just want to get off with Jane. If that had been Norman or Rita asking whether you wanted to go, I bet you'd have said no."

"Nonsense. I think it's very important that I learn about law and local government and other things. I've always said that there should be more training for us."

"Did you bollocks."

Chrissy was becoming a little too fond of using that word I thought to myself….even if what she was saying was true.

Clive's response when asked if he too wished to take part in the NCTJ scheme was tersely negative.

At home that night I began to fantasise about sharing desks and drinks and sleeping accommodation with Jane in mansion-type edifices of learning in rolling acres of beautifully tended gardens and lawns.

A week later, confirmation of my placement on the course was sent through from head office. I opened the envelope. "Luton!? A day release course at bloody Luton Tech. Hell's bloody teeth."

"Well, at least you'll be with Jane…..that'll be a consolation," said Chrissy helpfully.

"No I bloody won't. She's down for a block release course at Portsmouth."

I honestly don't know why Clive, Chrissy and Janet felt it necessary to start laughing; I failed to see any humour in the situation.

Harry, predictably put his foot down and ordered me not to absent myself from the office. "You'll get all the training you need from me. Is that clear?"

And so it was that every Friday morning from the autumn of 1966 to spring 1967 saw me and Brian Dixon bombing up the M1 to junction 10. Brian was a nice bloke. Very knowledgeable. But banter was not his strong point and his interest in football, or at least my chuntering on about Watford, was not strong, so the journeys were undertaken mainly in silence. So neither of us were bubbling over with enthusiasm as we tackled the stairs of an unbecoming 1950s tower block to start on the day's lessons.

The one bright spot of the Friday experiences was sitting next to Peter Daniels from the Herts Advertiser, a 17-year-old with a silly giggle who took delight in asking bogus questions of the strait laced female shorthand teacher. Blimey, I thought, that's a bit juvenile. It's just like being back at school, taking the piss out of the teacher.... I think I'll have to give him a hand. Thus a friendship based on a mutual quest for low grade puerility was born. We were put together because both of us had a smattering of shorthand whereas the others in the group were absolute beginners. The tutor used to go on at some considerable length about the wonders of the system devised by Isaac Pitman in 1837 and how it was possible to achieve speeds of over 300 words a minute.

And so we entered the world of stee loops, ster loops, shun hooks and dipthongs and slowly developed the skills necessary to jot down what people were saying in a series of neatly placed angled strokes, curves, circles, hooks - and long words that we couldn't think of the outlines for.

The other sessions faced by students included current affairs, practical journalism, local government, English language and law. But arguably shorthand was the most important skill young reporters had to learn: not only was it essential for recording what was being said but without a 100 words per minute certificate, a National Council for the Training of Journalists Proficiency qualification could not be attained no matter how brilliant the student was with other subjects.

Peter and I hooked up together socially and regularly hit the R & B hot spots of London such as The Marquee to see the likes of Fleetwood Mac and The Yardbirds. He was on the sports desk of the Herts Ad and his ambition was to be a top sports writer; he clearly was not comfortable with the local government element of the course.

"Wouldn't know a parish council if one bit me up the arse," he said after we'd taken the end of year exams. "I've never had to cover a single meeting. I couldn't answer the question about the differences between a county council and a rural district council and the services they provide."

I murmured some trite drivel about eventually getting the hang of it, but he was confident that he had failed the exam. And he had, a point that was quickly seized upon by Mum when we called in at Berkhamsted on our way to London.

He had barely got over the threshold when she cheerily greeted him with the words: "Hello, Peter. Hear you failed the local government exam."

She beamed as she added: "Paul passed you know. Still, you can always sit them again, can't you. Cup of tea?"

I couldn't believe what I was hearing. Then it struck me. She had never got over my piss-poor GCE 'O' level results; not because I only got two passes but that "David (David Taylor Jones, my best mate at school and son of my mother's close friend Olive) got five or six, so why didn't you?".

"Sorry about that, Pete," I said as we drove off towards the A41. "I'd never have mentioned it if I knew she was going to come out with that."

He shot me a glance suggesting that he didn't entirely believe me, but graciously responded by saying something like "well, that's mums for you".

He duly re-sat, and passed, local government and our friendship continued as we graduated to the second year's training; a six-week block release course at Harlow starting in February 1968. We were joined by Keith Cheeseborough from the Gazette's sports desk.

After a short stay in a small semi with no running hot water or door to my bedroom, I transferred to Pete's digs which were owned by a distant relative of his who failed to appreciate our roughing up her garden with ill-aimed kicks of the football we'd acquired. Keith was billeted with a middle-aged couple, the male half of which delighted in cracking his one and only gag to Keith on a nightly basis: "You see that paint on the wall? That's Durex that is! Ha, ha, ha...."

Our main journalism lecturer was the first tutor I'd come across who had come through the newspaper ranks. Bob James, formerly of the highly regarded Northern Echo, was hugely popular with the students principally because he was such a good journalist and, he knew how to teach.

Like others on the course I was in awe of Bob and desperately wanted him to approve my copy. In the early days, however, my work failed to win any plaudits. Back it would come with blue pencil corrections and deletions.

When I started to bleat, he responded just sufficiently to allow me to retain a miniscule degree of ego along the lines of: "Paul. You get the facts in the story, but yer intros are too long and too bloody flowery. It's quality, not quantity. Remember, you've got to capture and maintain interest in your news stories."

What made matters worse was the realisation not only that he was right but that I had been churning out stories for the good people of Berkhamsted for the best part of two years that had flowery long intros...and flowery long middle and concluding paragraphs. I had managed with very little assistance to turn potentially good stories into boring essays.

"Ah, bollocks. Just pack the whole bloody thing in. If I'm that crap I might as well do something else." These words were said to thin air. I couldn't tell Peter about what I was feeling; my ego couldn't stand it. What an idiot. Peter was the first person I should have told.

My demeanour was not helped when I heard (falsely as it turned out) that Jane was dating Clive. How could she? Doesn't she know how I feel about her? Well, actually she didn't know how I felt about her as I hadn't tell her.

Actually Peter unwittingly helped prevent my disappearing from the world of journalism by stationing himself on the outskirts of St Albans where I'd pick him up every Monday morning on my way to Harlow from Berkhamsted. I could hardly just not turn up. And his comic commentary on what had happened in the football league over the weekend was enough to lift my spirits.

Our first session on Mondays was usually with Bob. I was not looking forward to it as I was not ready for another dollop of critical analysis of my copy or the dreaded 'running story' exercise which we were due to undertake. The running story is where a news story is active, continually unfolds with differing points of emphasis and the reporter is required to keep up with the changes and, if necessary, re-write the whole piece in time to meet a rapidly approaching deadline. The exercise Bob created for us was based on an actual event - the 1964 train crash at Nantwich station, Cheshire. On June 25, the 6.35am Plymouth to Manchester express crashed through the level crossing gates and smashed into the rear of a milk tanker. Basic facts involving timing of incident, numbers of passengers and early reports of damage were distributed and we started writing knowing that we had thirty minutes in which to complete the exercise.. No sooner had we more or less completed the task, Bob came in with an update that the driver and fireman in the train cab had been slightly injured and the tanker's 1,500 gallons of milk had gushed on to the track. Okay, so it was tricky but not too difficult to work the copy around and re-type a new story. 'This isn't as bad as I'd anticipated. I'm quite enjoying this,' I thought.

Just as we believed the running story had nowhere else to run, Bob hit us with another update; the tanker had been pushed into a Ford Zephyr which was in turn crushed against the level crossing gate post. There were two people in the car. No names or details of injuries.

'Right. Another re-write. Fairly straightforward. Phew this is tough.' Time was ticking on, though and the copy had to be ready in ten minutes.

As I finished the latest re-write Bob came in with news that the tanker driver had been taken to hospital, but that his injuries were not thought to be serious. Still nothing on the couple in the car. Out came the old copy paper and in went a new piece and the keys were hit hard and not always accurately.

As we ferociously re-wrote the copy, the deadline drew nearer. I had almost finished when Bob popped in and breezily announced: "Just had word that car driver is George Eardly VC, a world war two hero. A local doctor has had to amputate his leg to free him from car. His wife is seriously injured. Both have been taken to hospital. Five minutes to go. Oh....and I'll want a two-deck headline."

Amidst the following protesting uproar, in which I wholeheartedly joined, I ripped the paper from my typewriter and started hammering out the revised story with its new intro. I just about managed to get it done as Bob called time.

"Okay," he said. "Welcome to the land of hard news reporting. Hand in your copy and headlines...."

'Shit. Forgot the heading. Um....er....what the hell do I put?'

The others dutifully handed in their work leaving just me with the paper in front of me.

"Ok Paul, let's have what you've got."

I madly scribbled the first thing that came into my head on top of the copy and handed it over.

"Shit's teeth, that was tough," I said as Peter, Keith and I settled down to coffee and doughnuts in the college canteen. " How did you get on?"

"Scraped home by the skin of me knob," said Peter.

Keith coughed out half his doughnut and I spluttered coffee onto the table as we rocked with laughter. We then exchanged notes on the story and how we'd written the intros.

"What did you put for the headline, Paul?" asked Peter.

"Rail crash - G Eardley maimed."

My two mates resumed their juvenile merriment.

"Wassofunny," I demanded.

Keith just about managed to croak out 'G', 'Eardley' and 'maimed' before becoming incapable of speech.

Despite the mocking of Peter and Keith, I thought my heading was alright in the circumstances. And I reflected that it had been a gripping, stressful but very exciting exercise and I had genuinely enjoyed the experience. And, what made things even better, was getting back my copy later that day and seeing ticks instead of blue pencil condemnation and 'well done, decent stuff, crap heading' annotated in the margin.

I sought out Bob the following day and explained that I had been feeling pretty low because of the poor quality of my earlier copy. But that now I was feeling more confident thanks to his comments.

"Well the running story forced you to stick to the facts, to keep it simple, keep it concise. You pulled it off. Now let's see you apply the same principles to your copy in future."

"Cheers, Bob."

I couldn't believe my ears. Here was one of the country's most respected newsmen complimenting me on a story. Maybe I was suited to journalism after all.

Chapter 15

In March, 1967 with Englebert Humperdinck topping the charts with "Release Me", the first North Sea gas being pumped ashore at Easington, North Yorkshire, and the super tanker "Torrey Canyon" running aground off Lands End causing widespread oil pollution of the sea, the Gazette put up its cover price. With the annual consumer price index inflation rate running at about 3.5 per cent that month, the Gazette cover price leapt by a whopping fifty per cent - from 4d to 6d.

The Gazette carried no forewarning; no excuse about rising costs etc. Nothing.

"There's gonna be trouble," I opined. "The punters aren't going to like it."

"You're right...they won't like it. But I bet they'll keep on buying it," said Janet. She was right. There were one or two grumbles but not much else. And the letters page on March 10, the week after the increase was imposed, contained not one message of protest.

Chapter 16

My off, non-on romance with Jane had continued throughout 1967 and 1968 which was hardly surprising considering an ill-advised alcohol-fuelled approach following the inaugural Press Ball which was organised by a group of local reporters, most of whom were on the Gazette's Hemel staff. It was quite a formal do with best suits, DJs and long frocks. The event was staged at The Pavilion in Hemel and many local worthies including the town's mayor were in attendance. There was music, a raffle, tombola, a buffet and a stand-up spot by 'That Was The Week That Was' regular Lance Percival.

One of the main organisers was Rita who delegated Ball-related assignments to junior staff. On the night itself, it fell to Keith to escort the recently crowned 'Miss Print', a comely brunette who had won a readers majority vote in a photographic competition run by the Gazette. Keith was not an ideal choice to chaperone Miss Print; he was not at his easiest with the opposite sex, preferring to seek out the company of horse race punters and football club coves whose conversation was sport, sport and well more sport.

"Aw no, not me. Get Melvin to do it," complained Keith.

"Certainly not," said Rita. "He'll be drunk in five minutes and be all over her. There'll be a scene, Melvin will throw up....probably on her dress, and she'll do a runner. Now that would not do our reputation much good, will it?"

"Well, what about Clive?"

"Same scenario, same outcome. Although it might take a little longer. No Keith. You look after her. Introduce her to the local bigwigs. And DON'T get drunk. Understand?"

And so it was that Keith was to be seen marching the aforementioned young lady round the tables and dance floor saying things like: 'this way dear', 'can I get you a Babycham, dear?' and 'do you want a sausage roll, dear?'

An hour later Keith and Miss Print's mutual misery was brought to an abrupt end when a local Lothario made her an offer she wasn't going to refuse and off they went into the night. Keith's relief at her absence was palpable: he bought a drink and found a willing ear for some of his racing anecdotes..

I arrived with Clive and Chrissy and immediately headed for the bar where I could observe what was going and who was getting off with whom. And there she was, looking a vision in a full length green/blue dress and carrying a feather boa; it was Jane.

'C'mon, Paul....go and talk to her'. I quickly downed my pint and was on my way when Chrissy, who must have been reading my mind, piped up: "Go on Paul...there's Jane. That's why you've come after all."

As usual I reddened at any reference to an association with Jane.

"Well you're wrong. I ....er, I um...came 'cos I wanted to see Lance Percival. Alright?" I was getting more than a bit annoyed at Chrissy's uncanny insight to my feelings about Jane.

"If you say so."

"Yes, I bloody do...!"

I stormed back to the bar for another pint. As I downed it....a bit too quickly...I began to regret my sulky outburst, not just because it was more than a bit juvenile but also because I could no longer seek out the gorgeous Jane without looking a dickhead. And not looking a dickhead was far more important than pride-swallowing when you're in the company of arch piss-takers.

Apart from some complaints about the paucity of the tombola prizes and a scuffle at the buffet table concerning the lack of buffet following a surge of interest from, mainly, Hemel reporters, the event went pretty well. Although I didn't get off with Jane, neither did anyone else as far as I could see. She spent most of the evening with one of her mates.

'Well that's something, I suppose' I muttered to myself as I forced a fifth, and 'the one too many' sixth pint down my neck.

As I staggered out of the Pavilion to find my car, the cold night air hit me like a ton of bricks and I felt the dreaded whirlies descend.

'Oh no, no....oh, shit and bollocks, no don't be sick.'

"Are you ok, Paul?"

"I..er, I er..."

I couldn't believe it. There she was. Jane. Looking fantastic, with her mate. This bloody would happen.

"I...er hello, Jane. Nishe to shee you. Do you, err...?"

"Do I what?"

"Aah, I err.. sorry...can't stop...in a hurry. Shee you."

"You sure you're alright?"

"Never better. Mush go."

She was actually concerned. For me. She's wonderful. My response was to stagger off as fast as my leaden legs would carry me to the nearby bushes of Hemel's award-winning water gardens where I very noisily chucked up. By the time the last Bill and Hughie had been negotiated and I emerged from the bushes, with nose, eyes and mouth all dripping various fluids, she had gone.

I realised that even if I could find my car I was too pissed to drive so I set about walking the five miles back to Berko, and only threw up twice on the way. Oh, and I slipped arse over tit on the canal towpath.

Chapter 17

Mrs Rogers was the lady to avoid. Once a Gazette staffer had met Mrs Rogers, he or she, would do all in their power to erase the experience from their memory and make a mental note to not see Mrs Rogers again if that were at all possible. She was a lady who created trepidation and concern whenever she ventured into a Gazette establishment.

But Mrs Rogers was the sister of Herts Newspapers MD Tommy Robinson and a shareholder in the company and thus had a position of some sway. Unfortunately for us Mrs Rogers believed she could write. And she would produce reams of hand-written notes to prove it.

Chrissy strode into the office, panting. "God, she's on her way."

Pausing only to collect her copy of The Guardian she dashed out through the back door.

I looked up from working on yet another 'local bride for Wigginton man' wedding story. "What's wrong with her?" I asked Clive as he started to put on his jacket.

"Oh....er nothing. I expect she's got an important lead to follow up. See you." And then he headed for same exit as Chrissy.

"Blimey. Where are you off to? What's the hurry?"

"Ah, em, I've got to pop back to Tring to...ah..check something with the Council clerk. Cheerio." He just made it through the back door as Mrs Rogers entered the front.

A tall women in her fifties, Mrs Rogers was wearing a hat that might have been seen on Ladies Day at Ascot in the 1940s. Her outfit was from the same era. Accompanying her on a lead was a little Jack Russell that immediately started to bark.

"Now sthoppit Reggie. Act nithely," she said.

'Blimey...she even talks like Tommy'. I tried to stifle a laugh.

"Hello, Janet. Ith Mithter Thymondth in hith offith?"

"'Fraid not, Mrs Rogers. I think he's over at Hemel."

He was and he wasn't. He was probably sleeping off a morning's hard drinking at home in Hemel; he most certainly was not at the offices of Hertfordshire Newspapers as intimated by Janet.

"In that cathe, I'll thpeak to Chrithteen."

Mrs Rogers was the only person I'd heard refer to Chrissy by her proper first name.

"Chrissy at the council offices."

"Oh, this ith too much. I thuppothe I'll have to thpeak to Clive."

"He's out as well, I'm afraid. But Paul's here."

"Whoth he?"

"Heeth, I mean, he's our new reporter."

"Alright I'll thpeak to him."

"Er...Paul. Lady to speak to you. Mrs Rogers."

I walked across to the counter.

"Good afternoon, Mrs Rogers. I'm Paul Barnes. What can I do for you?"

"Here," she said, and handed me a pile of about 35 sheets of copy paper. "Thtype it up and ensthure it all gothe in next weekth paper."

"What is it exactly?"

"Ith my review of the BAODS producthsion of Blithe Sthpirit."

"What...all of it?"

"Of courth all of it. Goodbye."

She left the premises with what could only be regarded as a flounce, dragging the dog who was mid-pee behind her.

"Christ, Janet. This is going to take an age. Look at her writing. It's barely legible."

"Now you know why Chrissy and Clive disappeared at a rate of knots. And you'll have to do it or she'll go running to Tommy."

I sat down at my desk and started to try and make sense of her spidery child-like scrawl about the Berkhamsted Amateur Operatic and Dramatic Society's latest production.

She started with the jaw-droppingly interesting point that "Everybody thoroughly enjoyed the latest offering by B.A.O.D.s, Blithe Spirit by Mr. Noel Coward the well-known playwright."

There followed the play's synopsis that "Charles Condomine is a successful novelist who wants to learn about the occult for a novel he is writing and so he goes to a medium who is called Madame Arcati who holds a séance at which she inadvertently summons his first wife Elvira who returns as a ghost that only Charles can see and hear and she wants to ruin his second marriage to Ruth and so she plots to kill him but only succeeds in killing Ruth who then comes back to haunt both Charles and Elvira and so Charles goes back to Madam Arcati to get her to exorcise both ghostly wives."

"This is terrible, Janet. She doesn't appear to be bothered by punctuation."

"Ah, well. This is where your subbing skills will doubtless come into their own."

I shuffled through the pages trying to figure out how to turn this pile of pooh into something resembling a credible review.

She had gone through the whole three-act play, scene by bloody scene. For example, act 2, scene 3: "Ruth and Charles are discussing Elvira's 'appearances' and how disconcerting they are and what can be done about it. Ruth says 'You're not to let her know that we suspect a thing. Behave ordinarily as though nothing had happened. I'm going to Madame Arcati immediately. I don't care how cross she is, she's got to help us - even if she can't get rid of Elvira she must know some technical method of rendering her harmless. If a trance is necessary she will have to go into a trance if I have to beat her into it. I'll be back in half an hour. Tell Elvira I've got to see the vicar. And then Charles says 'this is appalling' and Ruth replies saying 'Never mind about that. Remember now, don't give yourself away by so much as a flick of an eyelid' and then all of a sudden Elvira comes in from the garden and Charles says 'Look out!' and Ruth says 'What?' and Charles, who obviously wants to pretend that nothing has happened says 'What a nice look out' and Elvira, who has misunderstood what is going on says 'What's a nice look out?' and Charles tries to cover up again by saying 'The weather Elvira. The glass is going down and down and down' much to the obvious amusement of the audience who laughed a lot."

And so it went on, page after page. After about an hour of trying to start, I did what any self-respecting, albeit cowardly trainee reporter would do. I put the whole lot untouched into the copy envelope with the rest of our morning's work and despatched it to Hemel via the 301c.

The 35 sheets of Mrs Rogers' bilge appeared as six shortish paragraphs on page three of Friday's Gazette: Suzie had done a proper job on the critique.

"She won't like that," said Janet when she saw the paper.

Sure enough, the lady herself charged through the front door within minutes of it being opened to the public. As soon I saw her quivering form appear behind the counter, I sped to the back door alongside the fleeing figure of Chrissy.

We returned a few minutes later by which time Janet had explained very sweetly to the outraged Mrs Rogers that I had dutifully sent her copy unchanged to Hemel. She kindly did not add that it was also sent untyped. Mrs Rogers was going to 'most strongly' take up the matter with her brother.

Chapter 18

Whilst the Gazette did its best to shine a light on local issues it was rare that we got the chance to report on international activities. One such occasion occurred in August 1968 following the invasion of Czechoslovakia by up to half a million soldiers from Warsaw Pact countries. Under the leadership of Communist Party First Secretary Alexander Dubcek and President Ludvik Svoboda, the country was enjoying a loosening of Soviet imposed restrictions such as on freedom of speech, media reporting and travel. The period of liberalization, which became known as The Prague Spring, began in the January of that year. However the democratic reforms did not go down well with the Soviet leadership which eventually decided to send in the troops on August 20.

Amongst the foreign nationals who were in the country at the time was a local student Richard Wardley. Richard was part of a group of visitors who were on a tour. I spoke to Richard shortly after he arrived back in the UK following a swift departure from Czechoslovakia by coach on August 23. Whilst he did not witness the mass protests and the tanks arriving he was able to give a flavour of how the country was reacting.

Under an overblown strap line LOCAL STUDENT IN A "RESISTANCE OF EMOTION, FLAGS AND SLOGANS" - and a five and two centred heading in 36 point Times Roman italic *In The Heart Of The Czech Fight For Liberty* over a double col sub head RICHARD WARDLEY SEES RIDICULE TACKLE TANKS, we were able to report his account in Gazette August 30.

The opening par read:

"RUSSKI IDETE DOMOI" means "Russians Go Home." Mr. Richard Wardley (22) of Potten End, observed these words daubed

in whitewash every 50 yards along the roadside as his coach sped out of Czechoslovakia on Friday afternoon.

In fact Richard, a Bristol University veterinary student, saw hundreds of similar anti-Russian slogans during the latter part of his fortnight's stay in the country.

The slogans - in Czech, Russian and other languages, including English - were splashed on the sides of buildings in the town where Richard stayed, painted on banners and printed on posters. Leaflets which were distributed by Czech youngsters carried the same message to the invader.

GENERATIONS APART *(crosshead)*

While teenagers too young to remember past oppressions openly revile and rebel against the Warsaw Pact forces, there are signs that Czechs of an older generation are changing in their mood towards the Russians. Gone is their characteristic numbed acceptance of oppression and in its place is a type of pacific resistance.

His own evaluation of the situation was given to the Gazette by Richard, a former Hemel Hempstead Grammar School boy, less than 24 hours after his return to England.

He had been on an exchange visit to Czechoslovakia with 19 other students and was speaking from his home, Brydens, Hempstead Lane, Potten End where he lives with his parents.

"Our party was drawn from the Rotary Group 109 Organisation."

He explained the first week of their visit was spent in a town called Zivohost about 60 miles south of Prague. The party then moved on to the capital on August 17. They left only hours before the invasion on Tuesday.

"We left in the afternoon to go to the youth hostel in Karlovy Vary, a town about a hundred miles west of Prague. The invasion started on Tuesday night."

LOW FLYING PLANES

"On the Wednesday morning we were woken by the noise of low-flying planes. We heard Czech loudspeaker vans going round the town.

"We did not know quite what was happening, but then our Czech guide came in and told us that a force had invaded the country overnight.

"She felt ashamed that as leader of the party she had to come and tell us. She was far more concerned for us than for herself. We felt sorry for her family and her fiancé who were in Bratislava.

Richard said that the party did not see much of the Russians. He said: "Two or three tanks did enter the town but we did not see them. But we did notice a couple of the roads had been cut up a bit."

THEIR REACTION

The reaction of the Czechs in Karlovy Vary obviously impressed him. "Students started writing 'Russians Go Home!' on walls in all languages. The visible resistance was from the younger faction of the community. They toured round the town in lorries waving banners and shouting 'Dubcek!' 'Svoboda!'

"Soviet plaques expressing friendship placed on the sides of municipal buildings were taken down. Even one on the side of the police station had been ripped off, obviously with the help of the police themselves.

"Those words of friendship that were engraved on the walls were either scratched out or covered up.

"It was a resistance of emotion, flags and slogans."
Mr Wardley described the immediate reaction of many of the older people to the invasion as one of 'stunned acceptance'.

"But," he said, "few of them have ever known freedom.

"However it was a tremendous shock as they had always regarded the Russians as their friends. Many Czech students had felt that the worst of the crisis about the reforms had passed.

MORE LIKE HITLER

"Most Czechs compared the situation to Hitler's invasion of the country and not so much like the invasion of Hungary.

"We heard nothing in favour of the invasion. I felt our guide was not a hundred per cent behind the Dubcek reforms before the Russians came to Prague. She did not seem to agree wholeheartedly that the reforms illustrated a true consensus of the feelings of the whole population. But after the invasion, she appeared to renounce her faith in Russia and in Communism itself - and was right behind the Czech Government."

Richard and his friends were kept informed of the situation by broadcasts from clandestine radio stations.

"There was only one time when I was a bit scared - and that was on Wednesday night when a rumour went round that Lyndon Johnson had said that if the Russians did not leave Czechoslovakia within three days, US forces would be sent in!

"The Czechs, however, realised that this would be futile. The problem had to be solved by themselves. Any intervention by NATO would unbalance the world.

"Their type of resistance - by waving flags and shouting slogans - was absolutely right. It made the troops, many of whom were under 20, look so stupid. It made the invasion look naive - a big blunder."

WHAT HE WAS TOLD

Although Richard did not see much of the invasion in process, he related a conversation he had with a Danish tourist who was in Prague at the time the Russians came in.

"He told me that he was woken up on the Wednesday morning by the sound of machine gun fire. Bullets were hitting his hotel balcony only a few feet away from where he was sleeping."

During the time the tourist was in Prague he saw two youngsters crushed between a pair of Soviet tanks. He also saw two citizens fall after a burst of machine gun fire.
"He went on to describe how young Czechs stuck flag sticks down the barrels of Russian guns and how many casualties were caused by bullets ricocheting off the walls of buildings."

The return journey across Europe was, needless to say, eventful. Richard's party arrived at the West German border town of Schirnding where they were met by a Russian Bren carrier and eight soldiers.

But they were not bothered and went through the checkpoint quietly. However, Richard noticed that the Czech border guards' Jeeps had anti-Russian slogans on them!

Said Richard: "Although I was glad to get out I was sorry to leave our Czech student friends and our guide. I felt in a way guilty at leaving them with such a mess."

Finally, what was Richard's opinion as to the outcome of the whole affair? "I feel the Czechs will always go on resisting," he said.

"They will never accept that the Russians' entry was a good thing for the country. The taste of liberalism and reforms will last a long time."

Chapter 19

Apart from the expected attributes of a local reporter - an eye for a good story, excellent contacts and an ability to listen and write clearly and concisely - there's another skill which doesn't get a mention in the NCTJ syllabus for aspiring journos: the ability to brown-nose. I learnt this vital skill when I panicked as a great local story seemed to be slipping through my fingers.

A 32-year-old local man had gone missing towards the end of August 1968 having sent letters to the police and relatives indicating that he was committing suicide on Berkhamsted Common, a beautiful but extensive area of woods and grassland to the north of the town.

We'd done a piece about two unsuccessful searches for the man and the story went quiet after police relegated the case to missing person status.

His body was later found by a man walking his dogs on the common near Ashridge College.

The local nick gave me the dog walker's name and address. .

"His name is Ian Payne and he lives up at Cholesbury Kennels in Bourne End. Anybody know him?" I asked when I got back tom the office.

Janet's ears pricked up. "Cholesbury Kennels....that rings a bell. Why do I know Cholesbury Kennels..? Wait a minute. I think we had a complaint from them about an ad they placed in the paper. Can't remember the full details but they weren't happy."

"Oh, great. This could be tricky."

I decided against ringing ahead as I didn't want a tongue lashing and an eff off over the 'phone.

Sure enough, the greeting I got from Ian was less than welcoming when I reached the house.

"Mr Payne? I'm from the Gazette. Can I have a word with you about the body you found on the common?"

What happened next wrong footed me. Ian Payne was unwilling to answer questions unless the Gazette paid a fee.

I half-giggled in a puerile fashion at the suggestion....."Oh.....you're serious. I'm sorry. I'll er....we don't um, er....we don't pay for stories."

Ian didn't appear impressed by my response and was certainly not ready to talk about his experience. Well not to me.

"Er....I'll ring the editor," I spluttered. "Can I, um, use your 'phone?"

I got through to Harry. "Hello um Mr Symonds. Got a bit of a problem. Mr Payne wants payment for the interview. I've already said that it's not our policy to pay for stories. What do you think?"

"You're right. We don't. See if you can get something."

"Er...ok. Thanks."

I hung up and turned by to Ian. "I'm afraid that what I said earlier is right. We don't make payments for stories."

Ian's body language illustrated all to clearly that we had reached a stalemate.

'Oh this is bloody ridiculous,' I thought. 'I'm here and there's a story to be told. I can't leave empty-handed. I've got to try and change his mind.' There was an awkward silence as I struggled to think of something to say.

"Um...I understand you had your dogs with you when you found the body..."

Nothing. It was clear he wanted me to go. Then I noticed his shotgun. He was obviously a bloke who went shooting rabbits or other game in the woods with his dogs.

"Are you any good?" I ventured. "I mean if you've got a couple of dogs....erm Springers are they...you er must be pretty good."

This was desperate stuff. I could feel myself redden as I chuntered on. "Do you shoot often?"

'How pathetic,' I thought. I can't go on like this.

"Yeh...."

Bloody hell. A breakthrough. I wasn't going to let this go. "I expect you're pretty good. Have you done any competitions?"

It was like turning on a verbal tap. It turned out that he was a very experienced shot and was a clay pigeon shoot champion. He was more than happy to give me chapter and verse of his shooting and gun dog training skills..

"Do you want to try?"

"What? With that shotgun? You bet!"

This was going better than I could have possible imagined. We went out into the long back garden and he showed me how I should stand and hold the gun against my shoulder.

"It's got quite a kick, so be prepared."

I was only going to be shooting into the trees, so couldn't do too much damage. I pulled the trigger. The noise was astonishing and the kick made me wince. Still, it got a grin from Ian who said something sympathetic about my shooting abilities.

From that point we got on like a house in fire and getting the story of how the body was discovered became a doddle. Ian, a 27-year-old painter and decorator, told me in great detail about how he, his Springer Nickel and her pup Coco were out on the common about half a mile from Frithsden Rise on the evening of September 3.

It was Nickel who discovered the body lying under a silver birch tree in thick bracken and ferns.

Ian told me: "I was walking along a bridle path about 200 yards from a field and suddenly Nickel started barking continuously about a hundred yards to my left.

"I repeatedly called her but she did not return so I went to see what the trouble was. When I reached her she was standing about 10 to 15 feet away from the body just barking at it."

He went on: "At first I thought it was someone asleep but then I saw that his hands were badly wrinkled and one of his fists clenched. His mouth was slightly open and lips were pouted and a blue grey colour. I then knew he was dead. The body was not concealed."

There was a strap hanging from a branch immediately above which had snapped.

The dead man's bicycle was found by police the following morning in thick undergrowth about 40 yards from where the body was discovered.

The story was front page lead on Friday with a terrific three column pic of Ian with his two Springer spaniels.

Chapter 20

Just over three miles north of Berkhamsted and overlooked by the beautiful woodland of Ashridge lies the truly picturesque village of Aldbury. With its village pond, carefully preserved stocks and magnificent houses and cottages, the village was and continues to be a magnet for TV and film producers. Aldbury hit the headlines in 1954 when an RAF Vickers Valetta twin engine training aircraft crashed at Tom's Hill just south of the village killing 16 of the 17 airmen on board. However, it was not normally a news reporter's Eldorado but there were occasional photo opportunities when film makers moved in. A scene from the WWII movie "The Dirty Dozen" shot in the village centre created a bit of a stir not least because as it required removal of television aerials from local houses.

It was usual for the Tring reporter aka Clive to do Aldbury stories but as he was away on holiday in early October, 1968, I went to the village for a routine job covering the shooting of an episode of "The Saint" which starred Roger Moore. The scene involved a scuffle at the altar during a wedding in Aldbury Parish Church (St John the Baptist). I had done a straightforward piece but Harry felt there was more to be had in the story And he was right. Instead of my pic cap story, we were able to get a page lead as, unbeknown to me, one or two locals had taken exception to the filming, feeling that the church was being desecrated.

Chrissy was also away, so we were two reporters down and after a moan about work-load from yours truly, Harry duly rang Ronnie to ask for the temporary loan of a Hemel staffer to act as cover. I hung around in his office to act as prompt.

"I need someone to go and do a vox pop in Aldbury on the Roger Moore filming piece that Paul has done," said Harry. "Paul can't do it as he's tied up with Berkhamsted stuff."

He frowned as Ronnie was being characteristically unco-operative. To Ronnie, Hemel was all that mattered. Berkhamsted, Tring and surrounding villages were optional extras.

"What do you mean 'me and my bloody vox pops'? There could be a good story there. I've heard that some of the locals are up in arms about the filming at the church."

I shot him a quizzical look. I hadn't caught any whiff of dissent when I was at the filming. But I wasn't going to protest if his ruse worked.

Harry could, when sober, be very persuasive and he eventually wore Ronnie down.

"Thanks, Ronnie. Can I have her here from tomorrow?"

He held the receiver away from his ear and grinned at me as Ronnie articulated his displeasure with the aid of many colourful profanities.

"Yes....and you!" He put the 'phone down.

"Well done, boss. Who are they sending?"

"Jane Attwood."

I tried not to react. I was hoping it would be Jane. I'd heard on the Grapevine that she was seeing someone which was a bugger, but I still harboured hopes that something of a romantic nature might occur during her forthcoming temporary stay.

It didn't.

Jane arrived the following morning without any hint of rancour at her sudden secondment. And Harry duly sent her out afterwards to do the vox pop of villagers' reactions to the filming.

"Now, Jane, I want you to try extra hard to find someone, anyone, to complain about the what went on at the church."

"I'll do my best, Mr Symonds."

As she left the office, I wished her good luck in what I thought would be a hopeless quest. She smiled back at me.

"Put yer tongue back in Barnsey," cackled Janet as the door closed, "or you'll catch flies."

"Oh, ha bleedin' ha," I retorted as aforementioned organ was returned to base.

Jane returned a few hours later.

"Any luck?" I asked.

"Well...a bit. Most people I approached were non-committal and didn't really seem to care one way or the other. But I did get one or two complainers. So there's enough to get a piece out of it."

Harry was doubly delighted with Jane's work; it meant vindication for his request to Ronnie and a better news story than I had written.

A Miss Burch, who had lived in the village for many years, had pronounced herself "absolutely disgusted" that the church was being used for the filming.

"The church is a most sacred place. It is God's house. Why should mock marriages be performed in our church?".

And a couple of other locals complained about the film crew walking over graves and trampling the grass in the churchyard.

Their objections enabled us to open the story in the Gazette 11th October with the question: 'Is a saint out of place in a church?'. The story and picture of a pipe-smoking Roger Moore signing autographs ran under a five and two heading in 48pt Tempo bold U & L **What's Wrong With A "Saint" In A Church?**

The star himself, unaware of the complaints, did his reputation no harm by sitting on a bench chatting to onlookers and popping into the village shop and buying sweets to distribute to children and their parents.

Within a week, Jane was summoned to return to the Hemel office. I had been on the point of suggesting a pint after work when I overheard the end of a telephone conversation which included the words: "......yes. See you tonight. Can't wait."

'Hmm....so the boyfriend thing is true. Sod it.' Other words of gloom came to mind as the self-pitying emotional icy sponge was applied. I had no proof that my assumption that Jane was in a relationship was true. But my state of mind at that stage left no room for doubt.

Over a pint with myself at The Swan that night, I gloomily practised my skills of flicking a beer mat from the edge of the bar on to the top of my pint glass. I'd actually got quite good at it: it was all down to the work I had put into the exercise over the previous weeks of lone drinking and brooding about why I had never plucked up the courage to ask Jane out.

It wasn't as if my reluctance was based on shyness. I'd had one or two serious relationships in my late teens and early twenties and a small number of fairly casual ones. It was probably down to a fear of rejection; I couldn't stand the thought of Jane saying 'no' and word getting round the Hemel and Berko offices that I'd been given the elbow.

I continued with the supping, brooding and flicking. "Done it! Yessss! The treble!" I exclaimed a little too loudly.

The barman looked up from his paper. "Done what Paul?"

"The treble. Three beer mats....one on top of the other. First time I've managed three."

"Well....well done you. Hope that cheers you up. Congratulations. Hold the front page!"

Ordinarily I would have responded to his sarcasm, but I just couldn't be bothered. I sank the rest of the pint, folded one of the beer mats in half, then quarters, ripped it up and left the pieces on the bar.

With the barman's "Oy!" echoing round the room, I left the pub and drove home thinking of Jane.

Chapter 21

Monday 7th October 1968 started like most of my working Mondays; in bed, playing with myself until 9.15. By now I had moved from Highfield Road, Bushey and was living in Berkhamsted. With Mum. She had moved into the lodge house that was located at the south entrance to Ashlyns School, Berkhamsted's sole state comprehensive. Elder brother John stayed on in Bushey. I occupied one of the two upstairs bedrooms of the Lodge which I was none to keen on keeping tidy. I always left the window open at night and during the autumn, leaves would fly in and line the floor. As they died off and gained the consistency of crisps, I could feel them crunch beneath my bare feet as I got up to go for a wee. Mum refused point blank to clear them up. Bloody cheek. 'Well I'm buggered if I am. She'll just have to put up with the noise of my feet crunching leaves. She'll break before I do'.

After the third shout from Mum that I should have been up and away by now, I scrambled into the pile of clothes left on the floor the night before, gulped down a cup of hastily made tea and jumped into my recently acquired Morris Minor. With the words from Mum, "For God's sake, aren't you at least going to wash?" ringing in my ears. I sped off down Coram Close and Woodlands Avenue in neutral without the engine on and kick started the car at the junction to join the traffic on the A41 and reach the office by 9.35.

"Morning Janet."

"Christ. Which hedge were you pulled through?"

"Thank you. And nice to see you as well. Any chance of a coffee?"

"Every chance. And whilst you're making it, you might like to know that Symonds won't be in at all this week – he's still on the course."

The course of which Janet spoke was neither educational nor golf-related; it was an alleged alcohol habit withdrawal course otherwise known as lying pissed at home.

"No change there" I muttered as I trudged towards the beverage making facilities.

"Anything in the post?" I asked more in hope than expectation that the week's lead story would drop into my lap.

"Just the usual twaddle from the WI and a crap poem from you know who."

'You know who' was a young local woman whose rhyming couplets would make McGonagall's works put Byron to shame. But they served the purpose of column-filling on slow weeks.

"No, Paul, it looks as if you're going to have to get off your fat arse and go out and get a story."

"Oh, bollocks."

She was right, of course. Since the advent of the Evening Echo, a November 1967 Thomson Regional Newspapers creation had started covering the area, the Gazette's news gathering prowess was taking a pounding: how could a weekly compete in hard news terms with a daily? Our stories had already been covered anything up to six days before we published. Our only recourse was to put a different slant on them or do follow-ups.

Or get things the Echo didn't.

The problem with this latter course of action was that it involved proper reporting; actually going out and finding decent stories rather than wait for them to drop in our laps.

I'd reached the stage in my career where the continuing round of weddings, councils, local societies, WIs and gymkhana events were beginning to pall. Reports of old ladies going on mystery tours and returning 'tired, but happy' and best potato prints by the worthies of the townswomen's guild just didn't cause the Barnes journalistic loins to twitch. Oh, for a decent story. And oh, for a decent exclusive. Now it looked increasingly likely that those twin ambitions would never materialise with the effing Echo creaming off the best stuff days ahead of us.

I trudged up to the police station to pick up the bits and pieces that were logged over the weekend. My mind started to wander about the likely items I'd be using and their headlines: "Cat nearly killed in near-miss road incident"; "Hole in road – police look into it"; "Man arrested for weeing against pub wall".

"Oh, shit. It's Monday, I'm fed up. Girlfriend-less and sod-all happens in this place." I continued to mutter miserably as I walked into the police station.

The duty officer looked me up and down, sighed and reached for the log. Yes, as expected, there was a list of low-level stuff involving missing felines, petty car crime, and minor road accidents – usually on the A41. Useful fillers but nothing to make a page lead until he added:"….and there was an incident at the canal near the bridge at Lower Kings Road. Seems that a youngster fell in and had to be rescued."

"Blimey. When was that?"

"Em….Sunday afternoon sometime."

"Have you got names and addresses?"

"Er….no. Nothing more than that. Well, nobody died so I don't suppose the lads felt it necessary to go into detail…. what's that Joe?" The officer was being addressed by a colleague at the back of the office. "Oh, yes. It appears the lad was rescued by some bloke and his son. Does that help?"

Bloooody hell. For Berko this was a belting story. I ran back to the office but before I could start dialling Janet piped up: "I think you may be in luck."

'What is she on about...she can't possible know already what I've just been told. Don't tell me she's got a name'.

"What, what...is it about the canal rescue?"

"No. I just had Peter Rost on the 'phone."

I groaned. Peter Rost was a local Tory who hoped to become MP for Derbyshire South East and was doubtless after some publicity for some non-story in which he could be quoted and, of course, photographed.

"Oh, what did he want?"

"He's hosting a meeting tonight of the Monday Club at Norcott Court."

Norcott Court was a fancy pile even by Berko standards.

"Well bully for him. Well I'm not covering it. Hardly news is it? They're just a Tory talk shop. I'll get Simon to pop across and get a 'photo and I'll do a caption story or something."

"You might want to do something a little more expansive, especially in view of the guest speaker."

By now Janet was grinning.

"Come on. Stop mucking about. Who is it?"

"Enoch Powell."

"Whaaat! Enoch Powell!. How the hell didn't we know about this before now?"

Six months earlier Enoch Powell, the then Shadow Defence Secretary, had been fired by Edward Heath following his so-called 'Rivers of Blood' speech on the subject of immigration which caused a nation-wide furore. Since then he'd been tracked by the media almost on a daily basis: there wasn't a more divisive politician around. Wherever he went, there would be a crowd of shouting supporters and opponents. The police were often in action breaking up fights between the various factions. And I'd regularly get into arguments with mates about Powell's views. "He's only saying out loud what people are thinking," was a common view amongst some of my peers. "Well he's not bleedin' well saying what I think," I'd respond. And from then the level of intellectual debate would rapidly deteriorate.

"From what I gather organisers were asked to keep quiet about it until today to forestall any protests," she said. "I've rung Simon and he's free to cover it."

"Christ. When I got up this morning I had nothing for this week. Now I've got two biggies. Thanks, Janet."

My first priority was to try and find the kid who'd be saved. First call was to the ambulance service. Had they been called out? Yes, they had attended and a boy was examined at the site but did not need medical treatment.

They had recorded the boy's name and address: It was Keith Saunders of 23 Ashridge Rise, Berkhamsted.

I hurried to the address and fortunately Keith's mum Joyce was in. She was delighted to fill me in with the rescue details and how Keith was very lucky that he'd been spotted in the water by a woman who found somebody to jump in and help him.

"It was a man and his son, I think."

"Any idea who they were?"

"No. 'Fraid not."

"So you don't know if the man was local? I need to find him you see….to interview him about how he rescued your lad."

"He didn't. It was his son who went in and rescued Keith."

Whaaat! This was turning out to be an even better story than I thought.

"It was his son…but why….er, I mean what was the dad doing?

"I don't know all the details, but from what Keith said, the dad couldn't swim."

I took a few more notes about her reaction to the rescue and got the ok to come back the following day to talk to Keith and get a photo of him. I then left to try and track down the young rescuer. The rest of Monday passed in a blur as I started to ring my contacts: local vicars, shop-keepers along Lower Kings Road, newsagents, nearby pubs. Nothing, other than the occasional 'yes, Paul, I heard about that. No, don't know who rescued him, though'.

I had to break off from the rescue story late afternoon to get up to Norcott Court where, hopefully there might be some action.

I found Simon at the gates to the house along with a small crowd of TV and, Radio crews and press reporters and photographers. "Where's the protestors, Simon?"

"There aren't any. I'll just have to get a shot of Powell with the Rosts. I know it's boring, but what else can I do?"

Clearly one or two people had cottoned on to Powell's visit as a few scrawled notices had been left in the lane leading to the Rost home stating such as 'To the Monkey Club. Aryans Only' and attached to the gate a sign: 'No Jews, Negroes, etc Keep out'.

About 160 Monday Club members and guests gave Powell an enthusiastic welcome when he arrived at Norcott Court.

Much to my disappointment and that of the rest of the media, the guest speaker never said a word on the race issue during his address, concentrating instead on how the tories should learn from the party's successful political strategy of 1951 to defeat Harold Wilson in the next general election scheduled for 1970.

Even the reporters' questions following the address could not entice Powell into saying anything controversial.

Although the story made an inside page lead under the main two deck across six and two columns headline **Enoch Powell Bangs The Drum On Pre-Election Party Promises**, in 36pt Times Roman, my opening paragraph was hardly an inspiration to continue reading: "On a day when anti-Enoch Powell demonstrators either lost their way or did not bother to turn up, the former Shadow Cabinet member was able to deliver a speech without the slightest interruption."

The nearest I could get to any discordant note was a quote from the Monday Club Chairman Paul Williams saying 'that despite the Club's admiration for Mr Powell, his views and those of the Club were not necessarily allied'. Wow that'll shake 'em up at Tory HQ.

After all, with an address titled '1951 and All That', even Powell could not have expected any major coverage of his utterances. Ordinarily I would have been disappointed with such an anodyne tale, but on this occasion I couldn't really get too disappointed as I was far more intent on getting THE real story of the week. I was desperate to find the young mystery rescuer.

However, the pattern of frustrating calls continued on Tuesday and I started to despair. It was like looking for a needle in a haystack. The incident had taken place on a Sunday, so the lad and his father may have been visitors. I couldn't believe that nobody in attendance would have the slightest clue as to the identity of the rescuer(s); not the police, not the ambulance people. At this stage, I only had half a story. Yes, it would stand up on its own and very probably a piece in the Gazette would flush out the rescuer. But it would also give the Echo an opportunity to chase it up and get the full story before our following edition. I even thought about holding the story until I had the identity of the rescuer, a course of action that risked blowing up in my face.

And then it happened. Salvation.

Janet answered the 'phone whilst I was making coffee. "Paul. John Lewis wants a word," she shouted. "He says it's quite urgent."

"John who?"

"John Lewis. He runs the post office at Potten End. I think he knows something about this rescue."

I dashed to the 'phone. "Hello, John."

"Oh yes Paul, I heard that you were looking for someone who fished a lad out of the canal. I think you need to speak to one of my paper boys, Graham."

Oh, there is a God.

A few hours later I was speaking to 13-year-old Graham Austin and his family. There followed on the Wednesday a trip to Keith's house for a re-union of the two boys, an interview with the 11-year-old and a picture of the pair shaking hands at the rescue spot on the canal. Unfortunately, I wasn't able to find the woman who had first spotted Keith in trouble, but no matter; that angle could wait for another issue. I had the story. THE story of my brief career to date. It was a story that just about wrote itself. It was a heart-warming, dramatic and heroic tale. But, would it be an exclusive?

I enthusiastically set about laying out the story, photo and headlines on the dummy front page alongside reports of The Rev John Gilbert becoming the father of a six and a half pound son and Berkhamsted Urban District Councillor Jack Rickard fulminating about rateable values at the authority's housing committee.

I was sure the Echo hadn't got the story on the Tuesday. But would they get it the following day? Or even the Thursday which would still give them the chance to scupper my exclusive. Tuesday night's Echo: nothing. Wednesday night's Echo: phew, nothing again. Thursday night's Echo? Would I open the pages to find a picture of two young lads and a dramatic canal rescue? No, I would not. Hallelujah and bugger my boots I had a scoop.

And there it was: the front page of the Berkhamsted Gazette, Friday October 11, 1968. MY story. MY scoop.

The four column 12 point Times Roman caps strap line read:
AFTER A "MYSTERY WOMAN" PLEADED FOR A DROWNING BOY –
The two-deck main headline beneath – 36 point upper and lower Times Roman italics of course – set centre over five and two columns:

Gallant Graham (13) Saves Life
Of Keith (11)

The 18 point Times Roman caps double column two-deck sub-head read:

DRAMATIC "LAST-MINUTE"
RESCUE FROM THE CANAL

With an opening par across two, the text read as follows:
A (Drop cap) YOUNG BERKHAMSTED BOY was saved from drowning in the Grand Union Canal on Sunday afternoon by a 13-year-old Ashlyns Schoolboy.

The dramatic rescue took place in the murky water by the locks below the bridge at Lower Kings Road, Berkhamsted.

Keith Saunders (11), of 23, Ashridge Rise, a pupil of Victoria School, was snatched from the water at about 4.30.

His rescuer was Graham Austin, of 5, Hedgeside, Potten End, who jumped in fully clothed. His father, Mr. Vivian Austin, a non-swimmer, revived Keith with artificial respiration.

Crosshead **MYSTERY WOMAN**

Keith could have died if it had not been for the prompt action of a "mystery woman" who was standing on the bridge and saw him fall in. She asked Mr. Austin for help. The woman's identity is not yet known.

Keith told the "Gazette" on Tuesday about his ordeal.

He said: "I had been to a friend's house and was walking along the canal tow path. I had just crossed over the locks at Lower Kings Road and when I got to the other side I saw a stick in the water.

"I bent down and reached out for it and fell head first into the canal. There was nobody about.

"I went straight under, but I came up again and managed to swim to the side. I tried to pull myself out but slipped back and started to drift out. I could not shout because I was out of breath."

A member of the Berkhamsted Air Training Corps, Graham was on his way back from an A.T.C. parade at Bovingdon with his parents at about this time.

He told our reporter, "We had stopped by the entrance to the football ground to pick up two of my friends when a lady came up to the car and said 'Could you help. There's a boy drowning in the canal'."

RAN TO THE EDGE

"Dad got a tow rope and I ran to the edge of the water. Dad yelled 'there he is, jump in and get him.' But I could not see him at first and then I saw his head come up. I was a bit scared.

"I jumped in and got his head between my knees; it was the only way I could get him to the side.
"I swam with one of my hands under his arm. Dad was dangling the tow rope and I grabbed it while he and Mum pulled the boy out. Dad laid him on his stomach and gave him artificial respiration."

Mrs. Pamela Austin, also a non-swimmer, explained that the unknown lady ran to the police station to give the alarm while some people from the nearby camera shop came out with dry clothes for Graham.

She said: "When the little boy's eyes opened his first words were 'Thank you for saving me'."

The ambulance soon arrived and Keith was taken home wrapped in a warm blanket. His mother, Mrs. Joyce Saunders, quickly gave him a bath and put him to bed.

FULL OF PRAISE

She was full of praise for what Keith's rescuers had done. "It was a very brave thing for a boy to do," she said.

The "Gazette" had some difficulty in tracing Graham – as neither Keith nor his mother knew his name. The police and ambulance station also had no record of the boy's name.

When Graham had been found, a meeting was arranged between the two boys on Wednesday at Keith's home. Mrs. Saunders' first words on seeing Graham were: "I want to thank you from the bottom of my heart for what you did."

She was not the only one who praised Graham. Mr. John Lewis who runs the post office and newsagents at Potten End – where Graham does a paper round – said: "He is an outstanding boy. It is the sort of thing he would do and think nothing of it."

Keith was back at school yesterday, looking forward to the afternoon swimming session at Ashlyns. "I intend to become a strong swimmer," he said.

As I had hoped, the story caused a bit of a stir and within a few days the 'mystery woman' made herself known to the paper. And the following week's Gazette described how Margaret Thorne, a 25-year-old nursery nurse of Curtis Road, Leverstock Green, Hemel Hempstead had been out walking with her mother and their dog when she spotted the accident. Not being a strong swimmer, she attempted to flag down passing cars to summon aid. Within a few seconds she attracted the attention of the Austin family who dashed to the rescue.

For his bravery Graham received the Royal Human Society Testimonial; the presentation of which was reported in the paper, alongside a picture, on May 23, 1969.

Richard Wardley of Potten End who was in Czechoslovakia during the 1968 Warsaw Pact countries' invasion. (Chapter 18)

Their Tragic Find Ended A Search

Mr. Ian Payne is seen here with "Nickel" and her pup, "Coco," the two English Springer gun dogs who were walking on the Common. "Nickel" was the first to discover the body.

Ian Payne and dogs Nickel and Coco who discovered body on Berkhamsted Common. (Chapter 19)

Roger Moore signs autographs in Aldbury. (Chapter 20)

Enoch Powell with Peter and Hilary Rost who hosted a Conservative Monday Club meeting at their home. (Chapter 21)

Canal rescue hero Graham Austin with Keith Saunders who he dragged to safety. (Chapter 21)

Margaret Thorne of Leverstock Green who witnessed canal incident and raised alarm. (Chapter 21)

"Beauty in Business" Suzette Couillault. (Chapter 23)

Helicopter spire lift at Ashridge College. (Chapter 27)

Round-the-world yachtsman Robin Knox-Johnston talks about his amazing voyage. (Chapter 31)

British and European boxing champion Henry Cooper at Berkhamsted charity event. He's pictured with, from left, Valerie Hine (18), Susan Barrett (18), and 17-year-old Jo Hanika. (Chapter 37)

FLP 'plane hijack hostages Rhoda and Margaret McGowan in Berkhamsted with Mum and Dad. (Chapter 38)

Tent dwellers Beatrice and Lucas Parker and their family at Brickhill Green. (Chapter 41)

Chapter 22

Not long after I started on the Gazette, I started hearing about a strange, forbidding, vaguely Dickensian establishment associated with the paper which was frequented by burly, surly journo haters. These were the black-fingered cynical souls who actually produced the weekly broadsheets, and a whole host of other items of printed matter.

And they were accommodated in a ramshackle edifice on the Leighton Buzzard Road known as The Works.

"What's it like?" I asked Chrissy. "I wouldn't mind having a look round; get to meet the blokes who actually do all that stuff with lead type and inky rollers and, er other things."

My knowledge of the printing process was, at this stage, limited to what my brother used to produce with his John Bull junior printing kit.

"You really don't want to know," she replied.

"Oh, but I do."

"Well….it'll be some time before you find out. It's pretty much like the forbidden city; at least for the likes of you and me."

"Eh?"

"The print workers are not like the rest of mankind. They have all these queer practices and regulations and rituals that we're never allowed to be privy to. They're all hide-bound by arcane union rules. Let's just say they don't really like us."

"But, they've never met me."

"Doesn't matter; you're the enemy. A reporter. At least you will be ….eventually."

And it was well over a year before I breached the outer defences of the works although I had occasionally delivered some late copy which was received with quiet loathing at the entrance.

The first thing I noticed when I entered the building was the smell….a mixture of dust, oil, ink and molten lead. It was the sort of smell that should have been bottled and preserved for posterity, for there was nothing quite like it. It was wonderful. Having only ever worked in offices since leaving school, this strange environment with its unique smell and constant tapping, clanking, clicking machinery was a sight, and sound, to behold.

Apart from the Hemel Hempstead Gazette, Berkhamsted Gazette and Tring and District News, the works produced a wide variety of printed matter from letterheads and invitation cards to books, brochures and posters. One of the major customers was the former Hemel Hempstead Borough Council.

There were monotype and linotype machines, the ever-bubbling hot metal kiln, racks and boxes of type being looked after by compositors, machine minders and those princes among print workers, the stonehands. At the heart of the works was the Cossor rotary flat-bed printing press which churned out 3000 copies of the paper an hour. Once this beast was up and running, nothing – apart from mechanical failure – would stop it; and woe betides any reporter who ventured close to the stop button. Most pre-print last minute changes were expertly dealt with by the stonehand rejigging the columns of type or shifting the pre-made picture or display ad blocks. Only in an emergency would an operator be dispatched to climb into "Gertie" as the press was affectionately called to unscrew the quoins, the metal wedges that locked the exceedingly heavy forme or body of type held in the metal chase or frame, to make the correction.

As time went on and I assumed more responsibility for laying out the Berkhamsted pages I became a regular visitor to the works and slowly but surely the attitude towards me altered from something akin to hatred to mere contempt.

When making up pages it was very important to ensure that you'd worked out the story lengths within the columns; running copy from one column to another was fine provided that the second column wasn't longer than the first. And if a story was too long to fit, the stonehand would merely chuck out the last paragraph or two. A story too short for the column was not a problem: the stonehand was armed with razor thin spacers or 'leads' which could be liberally slipped between the lines of type to fill the gap. If that failed, he could slot in the "There were no fires in Tring" copy from the previous week's paper. (If a column needed very little spacing, strips of paper or card were used: the printers' technical term for which was 'bodging'.)

When I finally got on talking terms with George – a prince among stonehands who could read the upside down and back to front type in the forme as quick as I could read text on a printed page – he consented to my entering the yard-wide strip that separated mortals from the stonehands' benches, to view his work at close quarters. On one occasion I was panicking that a name I had used in a report was wrong and it was too late to get the line re-set.

"No problem," smiled George. "I'll batter it."

"What's that?" I asked, breathing a sigh of relief as I waited to see how this experienced and expert craftsman would bring his skills to bear.

"You'll see."

One mallet, one chisel, one bang and sure enough, the offending piece of type was brutally defaced.

"Now that's battering...."

In a 24-page paper there would normally be 10 pages of adverts ranging from small classifieds to full page displays. The ad pages were made up starting from the back with the first (and final) page being filled with a combination of lineage – births and deaths – ads and news stories.

One stonehand was responsible for the classified advertising pages and the other for the news pages. The classified ad stonehand's work on a new edition of the paper started on a Friday immediately after the print run for the previous Gazette had finished and the formes dismantled and broken up or 'dissed'. When all the unwanted ads were removed – with the linotype 'slugs' (solid lines of type) melted and the larger sizes of single types, used for headlines and display adverts placed back into their respective type cases for future use – the resulting space was measured using a length of string to provide the essential information to help forecast the size of the next paper. Similarly the news pages' stonehand would diss the previous paper's formes and recycle the copy type via the cauldron and file the headline single types.

In the Gazette's hot metal days, it was usually the responsibility of the stonehands to determine the design of internal and non-feature pages, and the choice of type.

The Hemel edition was the first to be printed – on Thursday might – with the 4000-plus copies of the Berkhamsted Gazette and Tring and District News following in the early hours of Friday morning.

Chapter 23

Perks on the Gazette were few and far between but an editorial initiative from Ronnie proved popular amongst the male reporters. It was a regular column headed 'Beauty in Business'. It was based on the laudable premise that good looking females could make it in the male-dominated world of business and commerce.

For the Gazette lads it was nothing short of a sanctioned licence to stalk women: we had the go-ahead to walk up to anyone we fancied and start asking personal questions. The way we figured it was, any girl who worked was fair game to our lecherous intent. Unfortunately we were unable to extend our 'search' to lookers in public service such as councils, clinics and schools.

One such targeted attractive damsel was featured in the edition of October 2, 1970. The caption next to the picture read:

"Garages, we are told, will go to a great deal of trouble to induce motorists to buy petrol from their pumps with stamps, prize money competition, fake bullet holes etc. But Hall Park Garage, Berkhamsted, doesn't have to rely on such gimmicks to increase trade, their pretty attendants are already a sure-fire attraction. One of the attendants is blonde haired June Cunliffe who lives in Victoria Road, Berkhamsted.

June, who is 18, is five-foot-two and has, you've guessed it, eyes of blue"

Another local lass who was subjected to our attentions was "Golden-haired, blue-eyed charmer Carol Ann Mead of Southbank Road, Northchurch."

Carol Ann was a secretary to a veterinary surgeon at the Cooper Research Station at Berkhamsted. We informed our news hungry readers that Carol loved meeting people and had a great affection for animals and that her grandfather was the Northchurch policeman. The caption was finished with a warning to any romantically inclined local males that Carol Ann "has a regular and burly young boyfriend.....who might have different views!"

And November 14, 1969's B in B was Suzette Couillault, who, we reported, "....is half French, likes art, drama, riding, poetry and going to parties."

We went on to reveal that the grey-eyed blond, who works in the accounts department at the Economic Forestry Group in Berkhamsted, has ambitions to be a model.

We left the bombshell to the final par: "Although she is nearly 20, Suzette won't admit to a boyfriend of any kind - steady or otherwise!"

Local journalism at its best..

Chapter 24

The rigours of journalism training held no fears for Clive; he wasn't going to separate his rear end from his chair to take part. It wasn't that he felt he knew it all or was arrogant - he was just, well, not very work-motivated. He was able to cobble together just enough copy to fill the Tring front and that, he felt, should be that: nothing more should be required of him. When he was in the office he spent as much time drawing silly cartoons, often involving caricatures of Harry in army fatigues at the controls of a tank or lying on his back clinging on to an empty gin bottle. Or he would grab the office broom and march up and down the office holding over his shoulder like a rifle in the manner of a 'Dad's Army' character whilst coming out with various Harryisms. The Christmas before Clive left we decided to decorate the office and Clive was put in charge of the balloons. He took to the task with hitherto unwitnessed enthusiasm, blowing them up and daubing festive scenes on each. What he produced was indeed impressive; all included the obvious features of Harry in a variety of Christmas guises: robins, Santas, reindeers and snowmen.

"You can't hang those balloons up, Clive," said Janet. "Harry'll go spare."

"He won't even notice them," Clive said. "You watch."

Sure enough, when Harry stumbled through the office to catch the four fifteen bus home he just glanced at all the decorations and mumbled something which sounded like 'merry chrishmush'.

That he had got away with such a stunt emboldened Clive to take even more liberties with his Gazette employment. His output became sparser and his excuses more and more absurd. I'm certain I even heard him tell Harry that the dog had eaten his copy. It was patently untrue on two counts: Clive had not done the copy, and he didn't have a dog.

Clive had been looking for another job and it looked odds on that he would be moving on either having been fired or that he had secured alternative employment. His major love was motor racing and when a press officer post at the Thruxton circuit in Hampshire appeared in the UK Press Gazette, Clive started typing out his application. Never short of confidence, Clive spent the next few weeks happily wandering in and out of the office giving Harry less and less respect, and even less copy.

It was inevitable that matters would come to a head. And they did the day Clive learnt that he had landed the job. He walked into Harry's office to announce his impending departure whereupon Harry responded not by congratulating him but by referring to him as "an idle bashtard" who would not be missed.

Clive's response that he'd rather be "an idle bastard" than "a drunken pig" set off a train of events outside the norm of orthodox office disciplinary procedures.

"Right, you bashtard. We'll shettle this outshide."

"Alright then," replied Clive."Lead on."

Janet, Chrissy and I watched the spectacle with a mixture of disbelief and joy.

Harry rolled up his sleeves, clenched his fists and marched out of the back door and down the garden path. Clive got to the glass-panelled door, paused and locked it. Harry turned and was clearly swearing as Clive started pulling faces at him through the glass door..

By this time the non-combatants were rocking to and fro with laughter.

Harry shouted: "Let me in, you yellow-bellied bashtard."

Clive, by now armed with the office broom, unlocked the door and retreated into the main office where he sat on the floor.

"Get up and fight you yellow-bellied, lily-livered bashtard."

"Drunken pig," was Clive's response from his prone position.

Harry aimed a kick at Clive who responded by poking the broom in his assailant's chest. Harry snatched the broom from Clive's grasp and aimed several kicks at Clive all of which connected with the step on which Clive was sitting.

The kicking, the swearing, the "drunken pigs", "yellow-bellied lily-livered bashtards" and the laughing lasted until the front door opened and a punter with an ad and a puzzled look walked in.

Harry returned to his office and Clive to his desk to read his motoring magazine.

Clive devoted his remaining few days of employment with Hertfordshire Newspapers to 'calls', filing his usual 'No fires in Tring' paragraph and even a non-story about the non-existence in the area of one of the 1963 Great Train Robbers which was headed 'Ronnie Biggs Not In Tring'.

Chapter 25

Whether or not Clive's departure had given Harry an added incentive to hit the bottle, I couldn't say. But it was clear he was spending more time alone in his office with his gin and Castellas. Copy that was taken into him for editing was usually left untouched and collected by Chrissy or myself in time to catch the afternoon bus.

If evidence were needed that his hitting the bottle was affecting his ability to function effectively, it was lying on his desk. A taxi had been summoned to collect our leader following a particularly heavy bout of refreshment and as he left I spotted a piece of copy paper on which he had written a headline for a story linking business and local government. Harry's attempt to head the story: 'The Business of Good Government' had proved too big a task. It was the word 'Business' that found him wanting. He had managed 'The' with little difficulty, but 'Business' was a whole different proposition as was the positioning of the word 'Government'. The outcome of what his brain was attempting to convey to his pen-holding hand was:

'The Busisisinness of Good Gov'; the rest of the word fell away diagonally in a spidery line before disappearing off the bottom of the copy paper

And his liking of a tipple or six was not unknown in the town. Legend had it that a local bobby, patrolling the high street late at night, on seeing the office light on and the front door unlocked had entered the building and called out to see if anyone was in. Not getting a reply he walked through the office to Harry's room and knocked on the door. On hearing some muffled noises on the other side of the door he strode in to find Harry lying under his desk. It took some time for the officer to rouse Harry from his alcohol induced slumber and help sort out transport home.

His absences from the office were becoming longer and more frequent as he fought a seemingly losing battle with the bottle.

With Clive gone and not replaced, and Harry absent, there was more work for Chrissy and I to take on. But within a few months Chrissy, doubtless fed up with having to do extra work without extra pay, felt it was time to move on. Without too much trouble she landed a job with a Buckinghamshire local weekly.

Even Ronnie accepted that there was a need to replace Chrissy. Her replacement from Hemel was Melvin Thompson. It was clear that Melvin was none too happy at Ronnie shifting him across to the Berkhamsted office where he would be obliged to do evening jobs which did not involve musical events. And I was not overwhelmed by Ronnie's decision. I had hoped that Jane would be seconded but Ronnie was against such a move saying that we'd be spending all our time 'up the common' whatever that meant.

Melvin came with a reputation for not being overly keen on work. Socially, I got on well with Melvin, but if he wasn't going to pull his weight, I could foresee a bit of bother. I hadn't minded the extra responsibility of looking after the Berkhamsted and Tring pages and enjoyed being given the go-ahead from Ronnie to do some headlining and page layouts. I learnt how to measure copy in single column inches (approximately forty five in eight point times Roman) to help ensure that stories didn't overlap with pre-destined adverts. I also started to use different fonts for headlines and I was able to get rid of what I, with my nearly three years experience, considered to be hideously outdated 36 point times Roman italic that had been continuously used by Harry since the invention of the Gutenberg press. If the story merited prominence, I'd go to 48, 60 or even 72 point Tempo (a sans serif face) bold for the headline. And if the pictures were good - and they almost always were - they would go over four or five columns instead of the traditional three. But it was hard work and we needed someone who wasn't going to piss about.

On his first day at the Berko office we went out for a liquid lunch.

"Look, Mel, I know you're not keen on the move," I said as we downed our light and bitters at The Black Horse. "But it won't be that bad. You do the Tring stuff and I'll look after the Berko pages. What do you say?"

"I don't really have a choice, do I?" he said, staring into his glass. "I mean, I've been on the paper as long as you have, yet I'm supposed to answer to you."

"That's not the way I see it, Mel."

"How do you mean?"

"I was hoping you'd handle all the Tring stuff without me poking my nose in. I don't want the extra work of looking through your copy."

"Well, at least that's something." Melvin had got a bit of a chip on his shoulder about people altering his copy at Hemel.

"And how do you feel about doing your own page layouts?"

"Bloody hell, are you serious?"

"Yes. Why not? I've been doing the pages for some time now and Ronnie's never said a dicky about use of type sizes or fonts. So as long as you don't go mad, give it a try. It takes a bit of time to get it right, but if you've got a bit of imagination and can count, it's a breeze."

"Count?"

"Yes, you know....count the characters and spaces to work out whether or not your headlines will fit. If I can do it, any fool can."

Melvin's mood was changing by the minute.

"Are you sure about this. I mean won't Ronnie start complaining?"

"Ronnie doesn't really give a toss about the Berko or Tring pages....I daresay he never bothers to read them He's only interested in Hemel stuff."

Melvin was a quick learner and within a few weeks we were arguing about whose front page was the better designed and which headlines had the greater impact; the weekly competition was a genuine spur to both of us to produce something worthwhile. My personal favourite was over a story I wrote about a coach blaze in Berkhamsted. Fortunately the occupants were able to get off unsinged. **Coach on Fire, Passengers Alight** read the 18-point bold u & l single column head. Mel's scoffing was proof, if proof was needed, that this was a damn fine heading.

There followed several months of competitive banter and mutual mickey taking which was usually confined to minor grammatical cock-ups that one or other of us had failed to spot before the paper went to bed.

But ....woe betide the one who committed a serious faux pas, such as a clumsy chat-up line with a 'Beauty in Business' interviewee or a crass question to one of our local boys in blue. The fall-out from such a blunder would leave the offender open to serious ridicule for weeks on end.

With me having home advantage of knowing the area and being in situ, I had accumulated more piss-taking points than Melvin, although he refused to accept the score.

That situation, however, was to undertake a devastating change.

Chapter 26

My dear old mum, Dee, for reasons that remain unclear to this day, decided, without recourse to inviting my opinion, to respond to a Daily Mirror appeal for photos of aspiring male models. She sent a black and white, head and shoulders shot of me and, lo and behold, received a positive response.

"Hey look at this Paul," she said thrusting the letter with its Daily Mirror masthead in my face. "You've been invited to the finals of the competition."

"Competition? What competition?"

"I told you...the one that the Mirror is running to find the next George Lazenby."

"George Lazenby..."

"Yes. George Lazenby.....You know the man who does the Mars bars ad on television."

"Yes, I know who he is. But I never entered any competition. How and why have I got an invitation to the finals?"

Mum rolled her eyes. "God knows how you became a reporter...you never listen. I told you I was sending a photo to the Mirror. And they obviously think you're good looking enough to become a male model."

Now it was at this point that I should have recognised the sirens and claxons going off in my head, ripped the letter up and scolded Mum for being such a silly flibbertigibbet. But having a ludicrous ego and responding to the words "good looking enough to be a male model", I reluctantly...well, gladly, nay eagerly...decided to accept the challenge.

The finals would involve an interview and photo session at the Mirror's offices in High Holborn. The interview would be conducted by a group involving representatives of the paper, a modelling agency and George Lazenby.

I had lied to office colleagues about the reason for wanting a day off to go to London. Fortunately nobody seemed that bothered about me being away for a day.

I drove up to London wearing my best casual clothes. Alright my only casual clothes. I was not alone. Mum had decided to accompany me.

"Don't for one minute think you're coming in with me."

She looked hurt.

"For Christ's sake, I'm 23. What will it look like if I march in with you in tow?"

Fortunately she saw my point and we agreed that I would meet her at a nearby cafe after the event.

Actually the whole occasion was quite pleasant. There were half a dozen of us joshing about the women we could pull if we won the event.

The interview went pretty well, I thought. Even my bon mot about male models being "pooftahs" (in my defence, PC had not been invented in 1969 - and I was stupid) went down quite well. Perhaps, on reflection, I might not have ventured the comment bearing in mind that George Lazenby was a former martial arts instructor in the Australian army and had been cast as James Bond in 'On Her Majesty's Secret Service'.

At the end of the session a gorgeous looking female asked me to sign a form.

"What is this for?" I asked the vision in front of me.

"Oh, it's just a waiver giving us consent to use your photo for publicity purposes."

"Oh, that's fine."

I duly signed and studied her exquisite form as she walked away. 'Hell's teeth, she's alright' I thought. 'I'll certainly put her on my list to call when I win'.

I wandered out of the Mirror building still fantasising about what I could be doing with her when the words "your consent to use your photo for publicity" came back and caused my brain to start acting like a grown-up.

"Oh, shit."

Stupidly I hadn't considered the possibility that the Mirror might actually publish a picture of me. In those days the image of male models was, well, iffy to say the least. And to be associated with such a profession was a passport to eternal damnation of ribaldry from anybody who could be described as a bloke.

I walked into the cafe where Mum was sitting nursing her third cuppa."How did you get on then?"

"Erm...ok. Thanks."

"Oh, come on. Tell me what happened."

I explained with little enthusiasm how the afternoon's events had unfolded.

"Well....what do you think your chances are?"

"Not bad. Can we go?"

"What's the matter, Paul? You seem a bit down."

"I'm ok. Fine."

I just could not get out of my mind the prospect of seeing my face in the Daily Mirror. I rationalised that if I won and they used my photo that would be ok because I would be able to leave the Gazette and make my fortune modelling underwear for Marks and Spencer. On the other hand, if I didn't win and they still used my photo....oh the consequences were too much to contemplate.

The next day, I bought the Mirror and peered nervously through the pages. Nothing. 'Phew', I thought.

Three days went by and the Mirror still hadn't used the story. I'd had a call from the paper to inform me that I hadn't won.

"Oh, er fine. Thanks for letting me know. Er....when might you be doing the story?"

"It'll be in tomorrow's paper," came the reply.

"Um...will there be a photo?"

"I should think that's highly likely as it was a male model competition."

I may have been a bit over-sensitive, but I thought I detected some sarcasm in the reply.

I got to the newsagent's and bought the Mirror. I rapidly turned the pages until I saw the piece. There it was. A picture of the winner and....no others. The copy was all about the winning guy and, mercifully, none of the other competitors were named.

"Thank fuck for that!"

"I BEG your pardon?!"

I apologised to the middle-aged lady who was buying Titbits and a packet of Spangles.

With the words "well really" ringing in my ears I jauntily walked down to the office. I'd got away with it. Nobody here will know.

Mel noticed the Mirror under my arm as I walked in. "Not your usual paper...anything in it?"

I tossed it over to him. "Not really."

As he turned the pages I saw the piece about the competition. "Oh, yes. There's some bollocks in there about male models. I mean what kind of ginger goes in for that?"

I snorted in contempt as Mel chuckled and walked towards the kitchen.

"Post's in," announced Janet. "I'll open it."

Thirty seconds earlier I was in the position where Janet greeted the postie with the mail and would have received it and would have had the opportunity to open the stiff-backed envelope addressed to the Editor; the envelope that contained the picture. The picture from the Daily Mirror. The picture from the Daily Mirror which was not the picture in that day's paper. The picture from the Daily Mirror which showed very clearly a grinning yours truly with five other aspiring male models and George Lazenby. If I had received the envelope I could easily have taken it to a place of safety and security and destroyed the contents with little fear of discovery.

But no. The buggeration factor set in and a clearly delighted Janet started reading - aloud - the contents of the letter which was really a press release about the competition with biographical details of a young Berkhamsted man who had reached the finals. My useless attempts to retrieve the malicious missive was greeted with hoots of delirious joy from Mel who just could not believe his luck.

The Mirror had clearly targeted local newspapers in the areas in which the competitors resided to get a bit more publicity for the event.

As Mel wiped his eyes, I finally got hold of the envelope. My face colour had gone from white to deep red. I started to tear the letter.

"Hold it, hold it." gasped Mel. "We'll need that for Friday's paper. I mean that picture's got to be front page. It's genuine local interest. You can't deny the readers the opportunity of learning that their local reporter wants to be a male model. I'll do the headline: 'Ginger Paul, The Would-Be Poser'."

I left the building.

Chapter 27

A journalist's principal objective - common to all reporters no matter how long in the tooth - is the scoop; an elusive commodity that arrives through a variety of circumstances. There's the lucky break, the overheard conversation, the being in the right place at the right time, the cultivation of brilliant contacts...the list goes on. For a small weekly like the Gazette, real scoops were few and far between. Yes, we'd get stories first but, thanks to the advent of the Evening Echo, we might not be the first to publish.

However, if there's a will to beat the rest it could be done as issue June 6 1969 proved.

Along with national, regional and other local papers, Radio and TV, the Gazette had been invited to witness a unique piece of airborne building construction. The spire of the beautiful early 19th century Ashridge College chapel needed replacing. The chapel is part of the business management buildings designed by the famed architect James Wyatt on the site of the 13th century monastery - acquired by Henry VIII for a hunting lodge and later home to the future Queen Elizabeth I. A new 60-foot fibre glass spire was to be lowered into position by an RAF helicopter, early in the morning of June 6, 1969.

"Bollocks...it's a bleedin' Friday," I yelled in frustration. "Just our luck; a great story like this and we'll end up publishing it a week after everyone else."

I stared at the invitation again......7am was the scheduled time for the operation. Was it possible for us to get it in? Surely not. In normal circumstances we would not attempt to stretch the copy deadline past early Thursday afternoon.

I rang Ronnie and explained the situation. Ronnie was the one in charge of ensuring all copy got to the works on time and gave the go-ahead for printing.

"What do you think, Ronnie? It would only mean putting back production time by about an hour or so."

The 4000-plus Berkhamsted Gazettes were always printed after the Hemel Gazette in the early hours of Friday morning. They would then be bundled up and lobbed into the vans for delivery to newsagents for about 9am on the Friday.

"What? For a stop-press par? You've got to be joking."

"No. Not a stop-press. A proper pic-cap story. On the front page of the Berko."

"How the bloody 'ell are you going to be able to do that?"

"If I lay out the page leaving a three-column by eight-inch space with a six inch single column cut in, I can write the copy to fit. I'll get Simon to get an early shot so he can beetle back to the office to get the pic processed. We should be able to get copy and pic to the works by about eight."

"Eight a bleeding clock. You must be joking. Tommy'll have a fit."

"Well, don't tell him. Come on Ronnie. You know this is a cracker. It's one of the few chances we'll get of stealing a march on the Echo and the others."

"Aw...I dunno..."

I could tell Ronnie was starting to take me seriously. For all his "wibble-wobble" idiosyncrasies he was a true local newsman. If

Ronnie said a reporter's copy was a 'mucking fuddle' it most certainly was. He had cut his journalistic teeth with a respected Hertfordshire news agency. But he was also a realist. His response to one of my whinges about a story I'd done being held over was along the lines of: 'Do you honestly think the punters are interested in your news story? All they're interested is in the births, marriages and deaths, weddings, court cases and the bloody silly ad.".

"Look Ronnie....what have you got to lose? If I can square the blokes in the works, we can do it. After all, it won't be the first time the Berko's been delayed."

This was true. The old Cossor needed constant care and attention to keep it running but occasionally there'd be a glitch and production would be delayed whilst one of the blokes climbed into the machinery to fix the fault.

"C'mon Ronnie. This is a one-off. Nothing like this has happened before....a chopper lowering a spire onto a historic building. It's bound to make the nationals. And we'll be the first to report it...the first. Beating not only the Echo but radio, telly and the bloody nationals. Just imagine..a weekly beating them all...."

"Alright, alright. Don't go on about it. Just do it. But you'd better bloody do it right."

"Thanks, Ronnie."

My next call was to Simon.

"Got a great job on Friday, Simon. It involves getting a shot of a helicopter."

Simon was about my age and had started on the paper a few months before me. He had bags of enthusiasm and a lot of talent.

He had a fine tutor in the form of Eric Taylor, a superb press photographer who eschewed the 'line 'em up against the wall and shoot' approach adopted by some local newspaper snappers.

"What's great about it?"

I described the job.

"Wow! I'll go and check the site to see where I can get the best angles. What time is it set for?"

"Er.....sixish."

"Evening?"

"Er...no. Morning."

"Brilliant."

"No complaints then?"

"No....it'll be great. Like working on a proper paper. Em...supposing it pisses down or it's very windy? What then?"

"Well...Shit. I never thought of that. Let's just hope it doesn't. I'll meet you at Ashridge a bit before six then."

"Ok, Paul. Thanks."

Blimey. Simon was thanking me for giving him a job that would require arising about four hours than he was used to getting up.

As the Friday drew nearer I started having kittens about the weather. I had been so wound up by getting the story first that I just hadn't considered the possibility of it being cancelled because of rubbish weather. What an idiot. I rang the college who confirmed that the weather conditions had to be reasonably calm to enable the operation to go ahead. A drop of rain would probably not hinder the job too much. But if it was windy....

I anxiously and intently listened to the forecast on the Thursday night and fortunately the predicted weather for our part of the country was not too bad. I went to bed fairly late, but didn't sleep at all well. I didn't need the alarm clock to wake me on Friday. I was up and dressed by five. It was an absolutely beautiful morning with barely a breath of wind. I drove on deserted roads and along the stretch on Berkhamsted Common that winds through gorgeous wooded countryside. The deer herd barely glanced in my direction as I passed the toll station that would, during 'office' hours be manned and charge a shilling to drivers wanting to take the short cut to Little Gaddesden

There was already quite a bit of activity; the helicopter had been fired up and appeared ready to take off. A crew had latched the point of the spire to the chopper's hatch. A crowd of College staff, students and locals were in position to witness the unique event.

I looked round nervously to see if Simon had arrived.

"Paul. Over here!"

I turned to see Simon's grinning face looking down at me from what appeared to be the edge of the roof. Christ, how did he get up there? What a great view he'd have of the operation.

"Blimey, Simon. How did you get the okay to go there?"

"Oh...you know..."

I didn't but wasn't going to ask. I just hoped that he'd got enough film and that his camera was functioning.

"And, yes....I have got enough film. And, yes, I have a back-up camera."

Photographers, especially press photographers, had to effect good humoured bonhomie when dealing with the daily 'jokes' of those in front of the lenses about the workings of their cameras.

It was just after six. I started taking notes about what was happening along with journos from papers, radio and TV. It felt great to be amongst such a gathering. Got the names of the crew and waited for what seemed an age for lift off. It was getting close to seven and I was already mentally writing the story. At last, at six fifty five the Wessex helicopter slowly rose from the ground and took up the slack of the 20foot-long heavy duty nylon strap that was secured to the top of the 35 hundredweight, sixty-foot spire. With Flight Lieutenant Stan Smith at the controls and Sergeant Fred Shoesmith sitting at the open hatch, the Wessex rose to about 200 feet and hovered over the 100-foot tower before slowing descending with Sgt Shoesmith yelling instructions to his pilot and the awaiting operatives below. There was only enough fuel for a single go at the lowering operation. Flt Lt Smith expertly manoeuvred the dangling spire to the point where the awaiting men could secure the fibreglass spire onto the tower top fixing points.

When I was satisfied that nothing could now go wrong - that the operation was a success - I belted back to my car and drove like the clappers to Hemel Hemsptead. Simon had left a bit before me to process a picture and get the resulting plate to the works where it was quickly affixed to a pre-cut wooden block. I went straight to the works with my typewriter and hammered out a 200-word story. It was a doddle as I'd already rehearsed several days before what I would record.

To emphasise the fact that we would be first to report the event I headed the piece "This Morning's Air Lift For Spire!" and opened with the words "At 7.10 precisely this morning....." with the word 'Friday' in parenthesis - just in case anyone should be in any doubt about the timing.

The compositor re-typed my copy into lines of lead pieces and handed it to George who slotted it into position The picture, headline and copy fitted the gap in the page like a dream and I got a thumbs-up from George, who gave the forme a shake on the table before tightening the screws of the metal chase and handing on the finished page for printing.

I was too excited to leave and watched the press as it trundled into action. As the first copies slid down the line for bundling I caught sight of the picture and story.

As one of my jobs was to scrawl shortened headings onto the posters that were clipped behind the free-standing billboards outside newsagents, there was little doubt what I would be selecting as the top item and, yes, space for the word EXCLUSIVE would be found.

Chapter 28

Having managed to scrape through the modules of the NCTJ journalism courses at Luton and, in 1968, Harlow, the prospect of the Proficiency Test began to loom large. There was, for me, a major obstacle to overcome in advance of the Test: achieving 100wpm shorthand.

It's difficult, and boring, to practice on your own and it was clear I was going to need some proper help.

I rang the font of all knowledge aka Wendy at Hemel.

"Hi Wendy, I need to get my shorthand up to speed. Do you know anybody locally who teaches shorthand?"

"Oh yes. Mrs Jackson at Warners End. That's who we send people to."

"Great. Can we do it on exes?"

"Don't be silly, Paul."

"Great. How do I get in touch with her?"

"No problem. Just pop along with Keith and Jane. They go on a Tuesday night. Hang on. I'll get Jane and she can give you the details."

I felt my pulse quicken. 'Jane goes to shorthand....oh, and Keith. Christ, I could be in here'. I hadn't spoken to Jane since my disastrous performance amidst the bushes of the Water Gardens. 'This could be my chance of redemption'.

"Hello?" It was Jane. "Paul?"

"Oh, er, hi Jane. I er... Wendy said that you and Keith go for shorthand shessions.....I mean shorthand lessons. And that I could go with you....er and Keith. Do you think that'd be ok?"

"Yes. I'm sure Mrs Jackson will be ok with you going. After all, it's another five bob for her."

"Right um I'll remember to ring the five knob, bob...bob....five bob. I'll bring five bob."

Hell's teeth what IS the matter with me? Why do I start talking like an arse when I speak to Jane? I'm sure I could hear laughter on the end of the 'phone.

I affected a silly cough to cover up my verbal boob.

"Um..er sorry. Jane. What time do you go? I mean when do I have to be there?"

"Seven o'clock."

"Great. See you there. Cheers."

"Before you hang up don't you want the address?" Cue more titters at her end.

"Oh...er..yes. Of course."

I couldn't wait for Tuesday. I started to fantasise about how I would ask Jane out. I'd have to play it a bit cool as Keith would be there. I'd invite her to go for a drink after the lesson. Yes, I could make an excuse about discussing the lesson and what we had done and I'm sure she'd agree. Trouble is, Keith would be there and I couldn't just ask Jane. Anyway, I liked Keith. We got on well and he'd expect to go to the pub as well. 'Well, never mind. There's bound to be an opportunity to speak to her on her own. Yes, she'll look at me and say something like, 'oh, Paul....you don't know how long I've waited for this moment...for you to ask me out. And she'll fling her arms round me and pull me into a fierce embrace and....'

"Paul....you forgot to pull the bloody chain." It was Chrissy. "I don't want to have to stare at your turds again. And bloody well open the window after you've been."

"Oh...er sorry." Embarrassing, sure, but I was still in Jane fantasy land and was thus not altogether bothered with the toilet faux pas.

Tuesday arrived and after work I rushed home to change and splash some Old Spice on my freshly shaved face.

'Ow...that smarts'. I looked at myself in the mirror. 'Bollocks. A spot'. I found a pin, dipped the end into some TCP and aimed at the centre of the offending mound. I had to jab at it three times before it obligingly opened to allow the puss to squirt free. By now I had something of a cut with a trickle of blood oozing. I dabbed at it with some toilet paper. 'That's great....she'll love that'. I couldn't envisage much embracing.

I arrived at the home of Mrs Jackson. I introduced myself and she said yes, she was expecting me and would I like a cup of tea? Keith was already there.

"Hi Paul. Got your pencil and notebook?" Keith was grinning because he already knew the answer to his question.

"Oh shit, no."

In the panic to dress my facial wound, I'd forgotten to bring either.

"Just like a true reporter. Ha, ha. I wonder how long this blunder will take to leak out?"

"Oh, Christ, Keith. I'll buy you a pint. Just keep your gob, shut. Em...by the way...where's Jane?"

"Oh, she can't make it tonight. Ronnie gave her a last minute job. She's got to go and cover a meeting in Apsley. Still...nothing to stop us going for a pint afterwards, is there?

My heart sunk and I swear I saw the beginning of a smirk on his lips, but before I could remonstrate, Mrs Jackson returned with the tea and we started to chat about 'L' hooks and 'S' circles.

"What speed are you, Paul?" asked Mrs Jackson.

"Blimey....er...about seventy I think. Not sure."

"Well, I'll start with Keith because he's a bit slower than that. Is that ok?"

"Suits me. Er?"

"Yes?"

"Have you got any note paper and pencils, please? I appear to have left my stuff at the office."

Chapter 29

After a few months of coaching at Mrs Jackson's, my shorthand, although untidy, had improved and I sat the 100wpm test and...passed. And so it was that I travelled to Debden House in Loughton, Essex with Peter to take part in a week-long intensive Proficiency refresher course organised by the NCTJ.

The course would cover the four elements that would be included in the final exams due to take place a few weeks later in November 1969. Peter and I were allocated one of a series of two-bed chalets in the grounds. There were a number of other familiar faces from the Harlow course who were also hoping to get the all-important Proficiency qualification.

And Jane was amongst the other students who'd attended NCTJ courses at Darlington and Portsmouth. She was paired with one of her mates from Portsmouth with whom she had travelled from Hemel. Keith did not come on the refresher as he had dropped out of training following the offer of a job on the Racing Post which did not require his gaining the Proficiency.

Although we were on good terms and had enjoyed post-shorthand stickies with Keith at the Red Lion in Kings Langley, I had still not summoned the nerve to ask Jane out, partly because I was uncertain of her response to such a request. I was also still very wary of having a romance in the piss-taking atmosphere that was all-pervasive at the Gazette. But here, away from the Berko and Hemel offices, there was a window of opportunity. I think Jane had been seeing someone, although according to informed sources - principally Chrissy and Rita - it wasn't serious. My recent relationships were short-lived and had ended if not by mutual agreement by at least some semblance of civility except in one case where, again emboldened by a couple of light and bitters, I embarked on a rant against fox hunting with my then girlfriend....at the annual hunt ball which I was attending at her invitation. She dumped me. I still don't know why.

The atmosphere at Debden was refreshingly relaxed. Indeed, for quite a few attendees the refreshments at the local boozer held more appeal than the night studying that was expected of us.

"Come on Paul," said Peter on the first night. "Unlock your wallet and dust down the white fivers and let's get a few down our necks."

I desperately wanted to come up with a reason other than studying to decline the request. I hadn't told Peter of my interest in Jane.

"I....um. I don't think so."

Peter immediately smelt a rat. After all, I had never refused a pint in his company.

"You ill?"

"No, no. Maybe I'll just, you know, get my head down...get a bit of work done."

"Whaat! Don't be a pillock. C'mon. I'll get the first round. You can study all you like tomorrow."

"Oh, no...you go on....."

At that moment I spotted Jane with her chalet mate going towards the car park.

"Oh, hi Jane. How's things?"

"Hello Paul....yes I'm fine. You?"

"Yeh...er great. Er,. this Peter. Mate of mine. He's on the Herts Ad."

"Nice to meet you Peter. This is Viv. We were at Portsmouth doing the block release. You two coming to the pub?"

"Well, I am. But miseryguts here wants to stay in and study."

Jane turned towards me. She appeared genuinely confused by my refusal.

"Come on, Paul. I've never known you turn down the chance of a drink."

"Ok. If you insist."

Now it was Peter's turn to appear quizzical....and a mite suspicious.

Viv had graciously offered to drive us all to the pub saying that she wasn't much of a drinker and would probably stick to soft drinks and maybe one or two glasses of wine.

Three hours later, Peter and I in our over-refreshed state staggered into our chalet. It had been a great night, and I had chatted, so I'm told, quite animatedly to Jane and Viv. Peter was in his element. He was entertaining all and sundry with his Al Read impersonations. The more he said: "We've supped some stuff, I say we've supped some stuff tonight" in a strangulated faux Northern accent, the more I laughed. I'm not sure Viv found it that funny; being sober in the company of the well-oiled is not a happy place to be. With all the jollification there did not seem much point in attempting a serious play for Jane. 'Ah well, there's plenty of time. I'll ask her tomorrow'.

I didn't.

The following morning, I managed to crawl from bed to the mini kitchen and put the kettle on.

"Cuppa, Pete?"

No reply. Peter, who was still in the clothes he was wearing last night, was flat on his back, snoring loudly.

I made two cups and put one down on the table next to his bed.

"I'm just going to have a tom....I'll leave the window open."

Peter mumbled something and turned over.

I looked at my watch...it was closing in on nine.

"C'mon, Pete. First session is 9.15. Get yer arse in gear."

No reply. The cup of tea remained undrunk.

I shook his shoulder. "Pete, for Christ's sake we'll be late. Get up"

Another incomprehensible mumble.

"Well, I'm going. I'll say you'll be there in a few minutes, shall I?

No reply.

Most of the first session was taken up by the tutor giving a general bollocking about noise during the early hours and the lack of preparatory work from the group. The previous night's excesses had clearly taken its toll; there was precious little resistance to the criticisms and plenty of staring down at imaginary notes.

At the mid-morning coffee break I returned to our chalet. I tried opening the door but it appeared to be jammed. I pushed hard. There was obviously an obstruction on the other side. It was Peter, lying against the door, still drunk, still asleep. I pushed the door backwards and forwards against the burbling immovable mass that was my pal, but to no avail. I had no alternative but to, well, leave him there.

He finally awoke at about 2pm and made his way shakily to the final session: a local government lecture.

He fell asleep, dribbling and snoring loudly.

During the rest of the course I actually applied myself to the work and, to my enormous pleasure, discovered that I was one of only three or four to have passed all the mock tests.

As my name was mentioned, I smugly turned to see a grinning Peter, who had not succeeded in all the elements, mouth the words: "Bleeding swot."

Never in my hitherto undistinguished academic career had I been so accused.

Chapter 30

Three weeks later on the morning of the Proficiency test, I was on Berkhamsted Station awaiting an early commuter fast to Euston. It was bloody cold and I was very nervous. As I awaited the train, I looked through some notes taken at the refresher course. As I had done well enough in the recent mock exams I should have been feeling reasonable confident. After all, I had not rested on my laurels and had actually worked pretty hard on revising to ensure I was in the best possible shape for the test. It was a lousy day, with rain peppering the platform. I managed to read through a couple of exam papers during the 35-minute journey to Euston. I walked out of the station to Euston Square to pick up an eastbound Circle tube to Farringdon which was just a few minutes' walk from the exam centre in Clerkenwell, As I neared the centre, I felt my stomach cramp with nerves. I was not looking forward to what lay ahead.

Inside, the examinees were grouping along geographical journalism college lines. I saw Peter and immediately starting rabbiting on about likely questions in newspaper practise, one of the four examination papers we would be facing. Jane and Viv were chatting.

"Hi Jane," I called. "Feeling confident?"

"Not really, no. Especially after the Debden disaster."

"Oh, come on. It was not that bad."

Jane had been one of the refresher course so-called 'failures' due to a major error in accurately reporting casualty figures in the interview and story module.

"How about you?"

"Oh, the usual butterflies in the belly."

"You'll be alright." She leant forward and squeezed my hand. "Good luck."

Blimey.

"Thanks. And you."

Peter, with his trademark silly grin and wink, nudged me.

"You're in there. Go for it my son."

"What do you mean?"

"Don't play silly buggers. You know full well what I mean. Jane"

"Er...what...er me? What makes you think I fancy Jane?"

"Well, don't you?"

"No....well...perhaps...I've never really thought about it."

"Oh, really?"

"Yes. Really."

He gave me what I interpreted as a knowing look which I found a bit irritating. His face broke into a broad grin.

"Ah, well. My mistake," he said with a follow-up trademark giggle.

We were summoned to the exam hall. The first of the four exams was the hand out; in this case a set of council minutes.

I quickly looked through the agenda items from apologies for absence to date and time of next meeting. The most newsworthy story appeared in a report from the council's recreation and leisure department concerning the local public swimming pool. Because of cuts in the maintenance budget, the department's options were: a, severely cut opening hours; b, close the pool and offer it for sale.

We had forty-five minutes to knock out a major news story and come up with ideas to the news desk for possible follow-ups.

The second half of the morning was the session that most of us feared: the interview. The idea was that pre-briefed interviewees with a script would answer our questions regarding an incident about which we would be given the barest of details. There would be a strict time limit for the interview after which we would go and write the story,

All we were told by the exam administrator was that there had been a major crime in a fictitious town and that we would be interviewing a police detective about the matter.

We filed into a hall which was divided up into individual booths, each containing a fake cop, a chair and a table and a pair of clipboard clutching invigilators.

I approached my allocated booth. "Hello," I said. "Can you tell me about the crime?"

One of the invigilators to whom I'd addressed the question silently motioned me to speak to the man dressed in a police uniform.

I apologised and repeated the question to the man with the blue peaked cap.

"What crime?" came the terse response. "And who are you?"

I reddened as I realised two significant rookie reporter's errors. 'Well that's a bleedin' good start,' I thought.

"I'm sorry. I'm Paul Barnes from the Berkhamsted Gazette and I was told by my newsdesk that there had been a major crime in the town."

"You're right. There was."

"Er...could you elaborate?"

"I could if you asked me the right questions."

'Bloody hell, he's tough'. "Em, er was it a murder...or a massive punch-up...or, er, or...a theft of some kind?". This wasn't going well.

"It was a theft."

I started shakily jotting down the man's responses. Christ, it then hit me. I hadn't even asked his name.

"Oh, er sorry. I forgot to ask your name."

"Yes. You did."

This could turn out to be the longest unrewarding interview of my career.

"Can you please give me your name?"

"Detective Chief Inspector Gordon."

"Is that your first name?"

"No."

Shit, I've only got a few more minutes. "Can I have your first name please?"

"Peter."

"As in Peter and Gordon....ha-ha...er."

"No. Just as in Peter."

I've got to get some crucial information.

"Er....how old are you?"

"Look, that's not relevant is it."

Oh, this is the interview from hell. As he looked down at his script I overheard the words 'jewellery' and 'brutality' from an adjoining booth.

"Was it a jewellery robbery?"

"Hooray. Hallelujah. We've got there....and with only five minutes left." Just what I need. A sarky copper....who isn't even a real copper. I then remembered the magic six 'w' rule: who, what, where, when, why and how (how doesn't start with a w, but finishes with one).

As I applied the rule, the information came thick and fast. He was co-operating because I was asking the right questions. He even gave me a typed list of the stolen items with an approximate value of their worth. The story involved an armed robbery of an elderly couple who got seriously assaulted for refusing to give the villains the combination to the safe containing the jewellery. One of the major aspects of the robbery was that the crooks had had the foresight to bring an oxyacetylene cutter with them to get into the safe.

The resulting story virtually wrote itself; with so many good 'facts' the trick was to get as many into the opening paragraph as possible whilst being brief.
I managed to get the copy written within the deadline and breathed a sigh of relief as I handed in the paper.

The lunch break saw most of us wandering to a pub over the road, chattering about the stories we had just completed.

"Oh, no...I didn't get that" and "the robbers used a what?" were among the anguished snatches of conversation as we sat down to eat. Peter, Jane, Viv and myself sat together. We all, more or less, seemed to have got the story.

The first afternoon exam was the speech. The organist from one of the local churches was making a public appeal for funding to buy a new organ. It was a straightforward story, but it was imperative that you got down what he was saying in legible shorthand; there was no point in guessing words, making up or 'telescoping' quotes - attaching lines from different sentences to form one sentence - as the notes had to be handed in with the 500-word story.

And finally, it was newspaper practice which included a variety of questions about marking up copy, types of headlines such as 'banner', 'cross-head' and 'strap'; and the meaning of terminology like 'drophead', 'indent', 'deck' and 'curtain'.

It also included a section initials and acronyms such as EFTA (European Free Trade Association), DD (Doctor of Divinity, not Double Diamond as Peter recorded) and laser (light amplification by stimulated emission of radiation).

And there was a question about newspaper industry bodies including the Press Council.

"What did you put for that?" I asked Peter in the post-exam resume.

"Always thought it was a crap body with no real power, so I let rip. I called it a 'toothless tribunal'. Yeh, I'm proud of that. You?"

"I called it a body established in the UK in 1953 to raise and maintain professional standards among journalists."

"You boring tit."

"Ah, well. I thought it appropriate bearing in mind it is a supporter of the NCTJ."

"Bollocks. I didn't know that."

"Neither did I. Just made it up."

"You pillock," he giggled. "Oh, by the way. I haven't told you, but you know I went up to Middlesbrough for a job on the Evening Gazette?"

"Yes."

"Well, I heard back from them a couple of days ago, and they want me."

"Great. That's terrific news. When do you start?"

"Possibly January."

"Why possibly?"

"Well, the job offer is subject to me getting the Proficiency. So I'll be crapping myself when the letter with the results arrive."

"We get them before Christmas, I think. Anyway, all the best."

"Yes. Let's meet up for a mutual celebratory drink....or a drowning of our sorrows."

"It's a deal. Remember to bring your purse."

We shook hands. Peter had done well at the Herts Ad. In the three years he'd been with the paper he'd progressed to become Sports Editor. We mingled amongst our fellow examinees and I sought out Jane. She and Viv were non-committal about how well they had done.

"You getting the train back to Hemel?" I asked Jane as nonchalantly as possible.

"No. I'm spending the night at Viv's."

"Ah, ok.....well. See you then. Good luck."

"And you."

Peter suggested that Jane might like to attend our celebratory/ sorrows drowning session.

As she said "yes, I'd like that", Peter for reasons best known to himself, gave me a discreet wink and thumbs-up.

I rolled my eyes to the ceiling.

We parted as he made his way to St Pancras to get the train to St Albans and I started towards Farringdon.

Chapter 31

Whilst I tried to forget about the Proficiency in the following weeks, the all too familiar gut wrenching fear that I had failed would hit me at least once a day. Nothing in the post Proficiency debrief with Peter, Jane and others led me to believe that I had made any major cock-ups, but I still kept imagining a negative result.

And the fears would not subside.

"Stop thinking about it. You'll be alright," said Mel as we made our way towards The Black Horse for our customary lunchtime snifter.

"Oh, I dunno....What the bloody hell's that lot doing?"

As we neared the Rex, crowds of boys from Berkhamsted School were making their way into the cinema.

I approached one of the accompanying teachers and asked what was happening.

"The boys are going to hear about Robin Knox-Johnston's round the world exploits," he said.

"Why the cinema?"

"Well....he'll be showing slides on the screen."

"What? You mean he's here? In person?"

"Yes. Of course."

"Why, if you don't mind me asking, do you say 'of course' ?"

"Robin's an old boy of the School. Didn't you know?"

"No kidding. Look, I'm from the Gazette. Do you think it would be ok if I joined you?

He looked around and thought for a minute.

"Hold on a tick." He disappeared into the picture house and a couple of minutes later emerged to say that Robin was happy for me to attend.

"Your lucky day," said Mel and predicting my next utterance added: "Yes, I'll get a snapper over here."

Fortunately, for once I had a pen and notebook with me. I entered the cinema along with 850 boys and staff to watch and listen to the heroic tales of this famed bearded 30-year-old ex-pupil who had become, on the 22nd April 1969, the first man to single-handedly circumnavigate the globe non-stop.

He had left Falmouth on June 14 1968 on board the 32-foot ketch "Suhaili", complete with food, water and 3000 cigarettes, as one of nine competitors in the Sunday Times Golden Globe race.

Two hundred and seventy days later, having sailed 33,000 miles, he arrived back in Falmouth to win the £5000 first prize.

Being in the cinema on that day was an absolutely spell-binding and truly memorable occasion, listening to his exploits and seeing the magnificent photographs he had taken.

The spread in the Gazette of November 21 1969 included the centred five by two by two column Tempo Bold headline:

**Knox-Johnston Recounts
Historic
Voyage**

and a four column picture of the great sailor emerging from the cinema
and an opening paragraph which read:

HANGING OVER the side of the boat half in and half out of the water photographing an approaching shark; being nearly blinded by acid from his hydrometer; almost capsizing in a storm; and getting a little drunk when he realised victory was his: all these incidents were recounted by the winner of the non-stop round-the-world race by Robin Knox-Johnston on Tuesday.

"So, what do you think? Scoop or what! Just goes to show what you can get going to the pub and keeping your wits about you."

Mel looked at me as I proudly surveyed the report on Friday.

"You're just a lucky bastard. And we never actually got to the pub if you remember. So you owe me a pint."

"Fair enough. Let's get to the Heath Park (the Hemel watering hole currently favoured by Gazette staffers). And who knows, you may be able to pick up a Tring filler on the way."

I easily evaded his attempt at kicking my rear as we filed out of the door.

Chapter 32

Just before Christmas the letter with the NCTJ heading arrived to inform me that I had satisfied the examiners on the newspaper practise and interview sections but had failed the speech and handout sections.

Romantically, it had not been a very successful few weeks since the Proficiency exams; my attempts to approach Jane were usually thwarted by circumstance beyond my control. One of the many reasons I felt unable to contact her directly and just ask if she fancied going out with me was that I recently acquired a black eye following an accidental nutting from an opponent in a football match.

So I faced the prospect of a season of good will and general happiness looking akin to Henry Cooper after one of his fights with Ali and, more importantly, Janeless.

Mum had watched me open the letter. "Well come on then...how did you do?"

"I bloody well failed; two of the four papers."

"Oh, dear."

"Is that the best you can come up with? Oh sodding dear?"

"I'm sorry. I only meant to...."

Of course, Mum was totally blameless, but my default position of 'when in doubt, lash out' kicked in and she was the only one available to be on the end of my tirade of utter unreasonableness.

"It's no bloody use you being sorry, is it? That's not gonna bleeding well change anything."

I stormed out of the house feeling more than a little sorry for myself. As I drove towards the office, I started shouting. "I've fucking well failed the fucking speech and the fucking handout, the fucking easiest papers."

The confines of my car, which again needed to go in for repair - another source of extreme annoyance - were comforting only because I knew my outburst would go unheard by the outside world.

There was sympathy, although not that much, when I reached the office and told them. I tried to get on with some work, but couldn't concentrate. The 'phone rang. It was Jane.

Ordinarily, Jane would have been the first person I would ever want to receive a call from. But not today. Before she spoke it hit me. Peter, Jane and I had agreed at the exams to meet on the day of the results for a 'celebratory' drink.

"Hi Paul." I could tell from the tone of her voice that she was in good spirits. She's passed. Oh, joy. "Have you got your results?"

"Yes I have. And no, I haven't."

"Oh, I'm so sorry. I thought you were bound to pass. I mean you were one of the few who passed all the papers at Debden. Which one did you fail?"

"Two."

"What?"

"Two....I failed two."

I was not enjoying the conversation.

"Which two?"

"Speech and handout."

"Speech and handout. But they were....."

"...the easiest. Yes I know."

"Well, I've had Peter on the line about tonight. Wants to know where we should meet?"

"How did he do?"

"He passed."

"Great." My heart sank.

"I don't suppose you feel much like coming out tonight, do you?"

Not feeling much like coming out tonight barely hinted at my mood. But I had no choice. I could either skulk and sulk at home listening to Mum's sympathetic musings or withstand the humiliation of being the 'failure' of the trio.

"No. But, I've got sod-all better to do. How about the Plough and Dragon at Leverstock Green. Do you want me to pick you up? Eightish?"

"That would be lovely. Thank you. Are you sure?"

"Of course. Will you let Peter know?"

"Yes, I'll ring him right away. See you later then. Goodbye."

As I put the 'phone down it occurred to me that Peter had not rang me to discuss the night's arrangements. Why? Did he have some inkling that I may not have passed?

"Oh, dear what's happened to you?" asked Jane as she caught sight of my bruised face. I'd been asked this same question countless times since the match and had run out of clever-clever quips such as 'I head-butted
the 301c' and 'you think this is bad, you should see the state of her'.

I mumbled and stammered my way through the circumstances of my multi-coloured injury whilst trying hard not to stare at her legs which were largely uncovered save for what appeared to be little more than a pelmet.

"Oh poor you," she said putting a hand on my arm.

'Blimey...that's the second time she's shown me some sign of, well, affection'. Don't get me wrong. She'd never been in any way cold or off-hand, but her feelings toward me had always seemed, well, just platonic.

I blushed as if I'd been caught looking over someone's shoulder at a lingerie ad in the Daily Sketch.

We drove off toward Leverstock Green exchanging small talk about the Berko and Hemel offices. I was not looking forward to the next couple of hours.

Fortunately the pub was pretty crowded with pre-Christmas revellers and there was a good-natured buzz about the atmosphere. I got myself a pint and a snowball for Jane.

"Hello Paul," said a beaming Peter as he marched over to where were standing. I was dreading his next words.

"Hell to live with is he?"

Jane burst out laughing. She tried not to. Peter joined in, relishing the impact of his line.

"Been rehearsing that, have we?"

"Ah, c'mon Paul. It's not the end of the world. Look on the bright side. You're here with me, and your gorgeous girl friend."

"Look, Peter, she is not er...my girlfriend. Right?"

"Ooops, sorry Chief. Just assumed....."

"Well, you assumed wrong."

There was an embarrassed silence which I felt duty bound to break by apologising for being tetchy. Paul's line was funny and I probably deserved it after the ribbing he had taken from me about being comatose at Debden and flunking his local government exam.

The general mood lightened a bit and Peter asked why I had failed the speech and the handout.

"After all, they were...."

"Yes, I know they were the easiest of the four and no, I honestly have no idea why I failed them."

"You'll re-sit them won't you."

"I'll have to...not least to shut you up."

My mood had been lifted by the company and conversation of Peter and Jane and the evening concluded with Christmas greetings and promises to meet again before Peter left to begin his new job in Middlesbrough.

When we returned to Jane's house in Hemel it was clear that her folks were still up and that two of her three sisters were also at home. I did not want to appear in front of the massed ranks of the Attwoods in my current state. I drove home cursing myself for declining her invitation.

Chapter 33

After Christmas 1969 and still stewing over my failure to get the Proficiency, I registered with the NCTJ to re-sit the failed sections. I still felt very frustrated about the failure as even with the benefit of hindsight I could not put my finger on where I had gone wrong.

'Bugger it. I'll ask if I can have the papers back to see where it went tits-up'. I rang the NCTJ office and explained that I had registered to re-sit part of the Proficiency and would like some advice. To my astonishment I was put through to the man - I'll call him Arthur Jackson to avoid embarrassment - who headed the organisation.

I explained the situation and asked if I could get a copy of my exam papers so that I could see where I had gone wrong.

"I'll do better than that," he said. "I'll bring them out to you and go through them with you."

"What? You'll actually come to Berkhamsted? You don't want me to come to your office? That's very good of you."

"Don't mention it. It'll be good to get out of the office and see what's happening at one of the papers who have seen fit to put their reporters through our courses."

We fixed a date for him to visit. I couldn't believe it. The top man from the NCTJ was coming to see me to put me right; to explain where and how I had gone wrong. I couldn't wait. For the first time in weeks I felt upbeat. Someone was putting himself out for me.

Arthur Jackson's visit was scheduled for a week before my re-sit in March. Couldn't be better.

I met him off the train and took him along to the office and introduced him to Mel and Janet; Harry was 'away'. After a cursory look at the current edition of the Gazette and some amiable chit chat about Berkhamsted, we wandered along the High Street to the recently opened Blue Jade Chinese restaurant.

A few more pleasantries over soup and I wondered when I should prompt him to talk about the matter in hand. It was clear, however, that Arthur was more interested in the BJ's extensive menu. He enjoyed a pleasant meal; I was getting more and more apprehensive with every mouthful about what Arthur had in his briefcase.

At long last - well after about forty minutes - he said: "Well let's get down to why I came out here today; your exam papers."

I'm not sure I wanted to look as he started to spread them out on the table. I expected them to be covered with blue pencil marks, crossings out and all manner of negative comments. They were my papers alright.....but, there wasn't a mark on them.

We both stared at the papers. Following an uneasy silence, I tentatively asked Arthur if he could tell me what was wrong with them.

He looked at the papers, turned them over, and then looked them up and down once more.

"Erm, I don't know. The examiner's comments were in the margins."

Another embarrassing pause.

"Er...what margins?"

"Um... they've been removed."

"Right."

To me the situation was a little eccentric but hardly problematical. After all, Arthur was the top man at the NCTJ. Numero uno. The expert in all matters journalism related. A man of vast experience who at a glance would immediately be able to spot the many mistakes I had made in my error-strewn papers. But the silence continued. I tried again.

"So, um, where did I go wrong on the speech, Arthur?"

I called him Arthur as he had invited the familiarity when I introduced myself at Berkhamsted Station.

He looked at the speech paper again. After what seemed like an age, he said: "Not sure you spelt the organist's name correctly."

"Is that it?"

"I can't see anything else at the moment."

"And the handout paper, Arthur. Where do you think I went wrong with that?"

Arthur was shifting about in his seat and looking at his watch.

"Er, without the examiner's notes that were in the margins, I can't tell you."

By now, I was seething with bewildered frustration. I wanted to say: "You're supposed to be the top journalistic man when it comes to training reporters and yet you cannot detect more than one fairly minor mistake in two examination papers. You clearly haven't bothered to study the papers in advance or speak to the person who marked them. This has been a totally futile exercise."

I did say: "Oh, right. Well thank you for taking the time to see me."

"Oh, that's alright Paul. That's what I'm paid for; to help young aspiring journalists fulfil their potential."

What I wanted to do was smite his dangling bits with a garden rake.

What I did do was shake his hand and say I hoped he would have a comfortable journey back to Debden House.

I re-sat the papers the following week. I think I did okay, but certainly no better than I had done at the first exam. I passed both.

In doing so, I became the first reporter on the Berkhamsted Gazette to gain the Proficiency. I didn't get a rise.

Although chuffed that I had passed, I didn't have that exhilarating surge of glee and pride that should accompany such an achievement. I even allowed a suspicion to grow that following the unsatisfactory outcome of our meeting, Arthur had put the word out to his examiner that no matter how good or bad my second efforts were they should be placed in the 'pass' box. Unworthy, I know, but the seeds of uncertainty had been sown by not getting any explanation as to what I had done to fail in the first place.

Chapter 34

"Hello Paul. You like cricket don't you."

It was Norman Peterson on the 'phone. I glanced at the clock and noted the 3.30pm time-line. I suspected what I would hear next would have been formulated in one of Hemel's finest ale houses.

"...er, yes...Why?"

"I'm organising a trip to Sheepscombe....that's in the Cotswolds, um Gloucestershire I think."

"Right."

I gesticulated a handshaking gesture against my mouth to a puzzled Janet who silently mouthed 'Norman'. I nodded.

"Are you interested?"

"When is it?". I desperately started to mentally invent reasons to excuse myself from this trip.

"Saturday week. I've organised a friendly against the local team and I need a dozen or so to go down there. What do you think?"

"I ...um...er Not certain I can make it."

"There's a brilliant pub in the village. It's 17th century. Terrific beer."

"I dunno, Norman, I er....I er."

"Most of us here are going; Phil, Keith, Ronnie...."

"Ronnie! You must be joking. The last time Ronnie did any running there was a bleedin' air-raid on."

Norman guffawed. He was a hugely likable bloke whose main interests centred on real ale and poetry. He had been round the block a few times and had recently joined the Hemel Gazette after less than successful spells with a number of other weekly titles in south east England.

"Well. He insists that he should be in the squad. And the girls. Rita, Suzie, Wendy..."

My heart started to lurch. The girls were coming. A chance to see Jane without looking too much of a pillock. Well, this put an entirely different complexion on the matter.

"..er...is, um....wassername, Jane coming?" I tried as hard as I could to sound disinterested."

"Oh, yes. Jane will be there. It should be a lot of fun. Can I count you in? I need to know numbers for the coach."

I took a deep breath.

"Oh.....alright, yes. I'll go."

"Good man. Don't worry about the gear, they'll supply bats, pads etc."

"How about whites?"

"No. They're not bothered by stuff like that. They're not taking it seriously. It's just a friendly. The main point of the trip is to enjoy the piss-up in the pub after the game."

The company of Jane, a laugh with the lads, a friendly game and a piss-up in one of the most beautiful parts of the country....What could be better than that? I couldn't wait.

As the trip date drew near, I found myself getting more and more excited. I started to fantasise launching boundary after boundary with team-mates patting me on the back as I reached a half century and Jane clapping from the boundary edge. I'd modestly acknowledge the acclaim with a slight raising of the bat and a shy grin. And then when they were batting I'd get a hat trick and take a flying one-handed catch in the slips, again to general acclaim. I wonder if I'd be able to sit next to Jane. Or would that be a bit obvious and set tongues wagging? Being a fairly young bunch of blokes and girls the piss-taking was highly competitive and very ruthless.

Nine am on the dot and I was outside the Hemel office where the coach was parked. I was one of the first to arrive. Norman was looking fretful.

"Everything, ok Norman?"

"Yes, yes. Get on the coach Paul. I'm sure the others won't be too long."

Keith, Roger, Mel and Phil together with Suzie, Wendy and Rita were already in situ, occupying seats to the rear of the coach. 'Bloody hell' I thought. 'I can't sit with them if I want to sit near Jane'.

I parked myself a few rows up from the group.

"What are you doing up there? Do we smell or something?"

It was the arch piss-taker Mel who was beckoning me to join the group.

"Oh, er, right."

I trudged down to the back and sat in an adjoining seat.

Slowly the stragglers started filing in; Ronnie - with a fag on, Roger, Billy, Tom from advertising. Norman got in and did a head count.

"Right. All here. Great. Let's go."

I felt the blood leaving my face. Where was Jane?

"Er....hold on Norman. Are you sure everyone's here?"

I immediately regretted the question. Within a millisecond the group cottoned on to the reason for my question with Mel - it had to be Mel - asking in a ridiculous high pitched voice: "Ooohh, Paul. Who do you think is missing Paul? Is it Jane, Paul? Is Jane missing? Oooh Norman, shouldn't we wait for Jane? Aaah, isn't that sweet. Paul was hoping Jane would open the batting with him."

Everyone...well not everyone...thought that Mel was very funny. The redder I got, the louder and more raucous the laughter. Christ, how did they know that I fancied Jane?

"...er.. no...er it's just that Norman told me she would be coming," I feebly responded. Norman shrugged with a blank look on his face.

Cue more laughter.

Far too late I realised I'd been fitted up by Norman who'd been clearly primed to mention that Jane would be coming.

I looked miserably out of the window as the coach pulled away. 'I hope it bleedin' well rains and the game's called off,' I thought as the sun emerged from behind the sky's solitary small white cloud.

The three-hour journey seemed to take double the time as our resident comedian managed to fill any silence with a reference to the absent Jane. At last we got to The Butchers Arms and piled in for a pre-match sticky or two. The Sheepscombe side was there in force and seemed a friendly bunch. Strangely, they seemed to be consuming halves and soft drinks.

Two hours and three or four pints later we lurched out of the pub and back on to the coach which followed the cars of our opponents to the ground. It was a beautiful run through glorious countryside up to the field which was on top of a hill overlooking Gloucester and the Severn valley. The pitch was in superb condition and had clearly been properly cut and rolled that morning. At the roped boundary edge was a fine pavilion with big changing rooms, modern shower facilities, a bar and kitchen. The score board had all manner of revolving panels and there were huge wheeled sight screens.

"Christ," said Phil. "This could be a county ground."

"Thashright," slurred Norman who had extensively tested the local brews. "Isshoosed by Gloshersheer sheconds."

"Whaat!?" spluttered Keith. "I thought this was supposed to be a friendly. What sort of team are we playing?"

"Only a, hic, only a couple play for er Glosh ...for Gloshersheer."

So there we were. Of the dozen or so Gazette men and women in an array of jeans, tee shirts, shorts and skirts, approximately four had ever held a bat. And there they were. Eleven men, all wearing whites, eagerly throwing the ball to each other and doing short sprints and generally limbering up in an all too obvious a fit, and sober, fashion.

The toss was won by the home team who elected to bat.

Keith, who had actually played for one of the Hemel and district sides, took the new ball. I'd been asked to field at a shortish mid-off. Ronnie was at first slip. He had a fag on and, unbelievably, a glass of bitter by his right foot. Mel was behind the stumps and the rest of our team at various points they felt appropriate. Suzie, Rita and Wendy filled the vital role of treble long-on, principally in order to continue the conversation that they had started in Hemel.

The first ball whistled past second slip and raced to the boundary. Four wides and much laughter were recorded. The second ball was straighter but shorter and a bit slower. The batsman eyed it greedily and nearly wrenched his shoulder in an attempt to land it in Cheltenham. His connection was horribly mistimed and the ball floated off the splice of his bat in my direction. What a dolly. I confidently cupped my hands in expectation of the ball gently nestling in palms. However, the beer I had consumed had an unexpected and belated effect on my co-ordination and ability to focus. Where, in times of sobriety I would have easily spotted one red missile coming in my direction, I was, at that moment, seriously under the influence of the yeast-fermented, malt flavoured, hops soaked liquid. My brain weakly attempted to convey to my eyeballs that they should revert to equidistance with the resulting effect that not one, but two objects were approaching. 'Which one should I select?' I mused. Fifty-fifty....must be in with a chance. As my hands closed in and missed each other and the ball thudded into my chest, I recognised that a catastrophic error had occurred. The laughter grew louder as I fumbled for the ball and hurled it at the 'keeper to attempt a run-out. He ducked and the noise reached a crescendo as the ball raced over the boundary rope with the batsman, still anchored to his crease, looking totally bemused.

The first over set a more or less predictable pattern to the home team's fortunes. Suicidal singles turned into leisurely twos and threes when the ball went near Ronnie. As the ball dribbled past him, he would put down his pint, giggle and break into a walk in pursuit. And when he finally reached it he was consistently unable to lob it to the 'keeper, preferring to hurl it back over his head or to gulley and, on one occasion, to cover point (Norman, semi-comatose) who missed it. That gave the batsmen a unique seven.

As the game progressed and our outfield grew weary of climbing down the hillside to retrieve the ball, it became increasingly obvious that we might not win.

Thirty humiliating overs later, the Sheepscombe team tired of clouting boundaries, declared on 243 for three. The three wickets - all outrageous LBWs - came as a result of some overly sympathetic umpiring.

Over tea, Norman's tactical talk went along the lines of 'the quicker we get this over and done with, the sooner we can get to the pub'. His pep talk worked like a dream. Our scorecard read 21 all out. Top scorer with five was Suzie who went in twice. I managed to get four streaky singles.

I felt very embarrassed at the pathetic showing and said so, but mine was a minority viewpoint. However, by the time a few more pints had been sunk and we were homeward bound I was leaning towards the majority view that it had been a very worthwhile trip. But on the coach home, Norman's suggestion that we make the cricket trip an annual affair was greeted with widespread derision and giggles from Ronnie.

Chapter 35

With the continuing absence of Harry and the lack of a permanent replacement for Chrissy, I was fretting about the amount of extra work I was having to do. I'd been on to Ronnie a couple of times about temporary help. He hadn't been very forthcoming. I rang him again with my by now familiar whining plea.

"We sent you Mel. What more do you want Paul?"

"C'mon Ronnie. We're trying to do the Berko and Tring papers with just two staff. Christ...you've got an army of reporters over there; surely you can let us have one."

"I'll ask around. Can't promise anything."

I recognised a Ronnie brush-off when I heard it. I tried playing what I thought might be a trump card.

"Look Ronnie. I've got the Quarter Sessions tomorrow at St Albans. I'll probably be there all day. It's a big one and you'll probably want it as a page lead."

"Don't try and pull that one, Barnesy. You asked for it. We'll cover it from here if you like."

Shit...he had me over a barrel. I'd managed to avoid doing magistrates' courts and Quarter Sessions since I started and I was beginning to get embarrassed at my lack of experience in this field. So I'd volunteered to do the next QS and I was bowled over to learn that it was going to include one of the biggest criminal cases to hit our area in years: a local gang including three brothers had been charged with stealing nine mail bags.

"Anyway," he added, "it's a Berko crime, so we might not use it in the Hemel paper."

"Oh, great. Thanks a bunch."

"It's a tough old life, isn't it? But I will ask," he said with one of his silly giggles as he hung up.

I knew what would now happen. He'd pop his bloody head round the reporters' room and just say something like: "Anybody fancy doing a couple of weeks at Berko?"

There would be a few hollow laughs, a couple of muttered swear words and a general murmuring of such responses as: "Rather lance a boil in me bum", "Shit...I'd have to do an evening council meeting" and "Bollocks to that".

And Ronnie would just grin, light up another Embassy and return to his room.

I heard later that amongst the negative responses one of the reporters said she wouldn't mind going across for a couple of weeks. It was Jane.

Apparently her comment drew a predictable howl of derisive chuckles, wolf whistles and smutty gestures with Ronny asking her 'why the bloody hell would you want to go to Berko?'

Jane had explained that she was more or less up to date with Uncle George and Children's Corner stuff and wouldn't mind getting a bit more experience of general reporting.

Her explanation drew louder guffaws and cruder gestures.

And Ronnie, joining in the spirit of the occasion, had said he was not having her spending her time up on the common in the back of Barnsey's car. He added that he needed her to be at Hemel because who else was going to get his fags and strikers in the morning?

And with another giggle he had left the room.

It was Wendy who'd been quietly writing up some court copy who had sorted out the situation. She had told Jane to "Ignore the silly old sod" and go over, and that she would square it with him later.

Wendy was the real power at Hemel. She was the office mediator, delegator, arbiter and was also very good at her own job. And she was scrupulously fair in her dealings with the staff, and Ronnie relied heavily on her judgement. In simple terms, If Wendy wanted something, Ronnie would inevitably comply.

She encouraged Jane to give me a call.

When the numbers in the room had thinned, Jane picked up the 'phone and dialled the Berkhamsted office.

"Oh, hello Janet. It's Jane at Hemel. Is Paul there?"

"Oh hi Jane....yes he's here. I'll put him on. Paul...."

"Yeh?"

She cupped the 'phone. "It's Jane. From the Hemel office. Wants to talk to you."

"Yeh, Right. Very funny. Who is it really? Mrs Rodgers?"

Word had got around the two offices that I fancied Jane. I looked at Mel who started to smirk. I wasn't in any mood for piss-taking, especially after my disappointing chat with Ronnie.

"Just tell her I'm out on a job."

"Ah well," sighed Janet. "If you say so."

She un-cupped the 'phone. "Sorry Jane; he says he's out on the job...."

I lurched across my desk and tried to grab the 'phone from Janet's hand.

"Give me that bloody 'phone!"

Janet released the 'phone after a couple of stupid proffer and withdraw manoeuvres.

"Er....hello Jane. How are you? What er can I do for you?"

"Hello Paul. Ronnie asked if anybody was interested in helping out at the Berkhamsted office. I used to go to school in the area so I know the town pretty well, so how would you feel if I came over for a couple of weeks to help out? I must say, I could do with a change of scenery."

I couldn't believe what I was hearing. Here was the girl I fancied like mad asking....ASKING...if it was ok to come over and work in our office. What a turn-up.

"What? You want to come over here? You sure? I mean....it's ..em, quite a way....er from Hemel."

"Yes, Paul. I do know. I used to do the journey every day."

"Yes, of course you did....of course you did. Em, how will you get over?"

"That's not a problem. There's a decent enough bus service. Do you want me to come across."

"Bloody hell...whoops, sorry. I mean yes please, yes please, er, um, yes please."

"Right. That's settled. When do you want me to start? Tomorrow?"

"Tomorrow would be absolutely fine. Thank you. Thank you. You'll be helping us enormously."

"I haven't done anything yet."

"No. I mean yes. Er...see you tomorrow then."

"Fine. 'Bye."

"Goodbye, Jane."

I passed the 'phone back to Janet who had a silly grin on her face.

"So, you'd better change into something decent for tomorrow, won't you," she said.

"Yeh...and you'd better shave you scruffy bleeder," said Mel, whose smirk had grown appreciably since the 'phone call started.

Janet and Mel continued their mickey-taking but I honestly did not hear what they were saying. I wandered into the kitchen.

"Anyone want a coffee?"

"Yes please," said Janet.

"And me," said Mel.

Three minutes later I returned to my desk with a cup of tea.

"Haven't you forgotten something," Janet asked.

"Hmm?"

"Er...coffee, white without?"

"No thanks. I've got tea."

I spent the rest of the day just thinking about tomorrow. I would be meeting Jane in the office. I would be asking her to do selected diary jobs. How would she react? Suppose she didn't fancy going along to the Berkhamsted Rural District Council meeting to write up five and six par stories about damage to fences caused by deer in Little Gaddesden or allotment footpath maintenance in Wigginton. And if she didn't like working on such stories, would that reflect badly on me? Would that harm my chances of getting off with her?

And then it hit me. In my Jane/fantasy confused state I'd forgotten that I wouldn't be in the office when she arrived; I'd be in St Albans for the mail bag case.

'Christ, it just gets worse. I'm bloody jinxed.' All I could do is write out a list of things for her to do and ask Mel to brief her when she arrived. I handed him the list

"What....no kisses at the end?"

"Piss off."

"Oooh, touchy."

Chapter 36

The following day, I got up early...for me, and by 8.30 I was on my way to St Albans. I wanted to be at the court long before the case began so that I could get used to such unfamiliar surroundings and chat up one of the police officers involved in the case for some background. As I had never covered a court case during my four years on the paper, I was very anxious about what could or, more importantly, could not be mentioned in my copy. I needn't have worried as just about anything said during the proceedings could be reported unless the judge made a specific ruling to the contrary.

The case involved a five-man gang and the crime was one of Berkhamsted's biggest of the 1960s.

My report appeared on page two of the Gazette May 1, 1970. Under a five and two column centred head in 36point Times Roman caps:
**MAILBAG THIEVES HID PROPERTY
IN LOFT**

it read:

"This is a shocking case: as bad a case as I have ever had since sitting on the Bench in this county," said Mr. Geoffrey Crispin QC last week before he sentenced members of a Berkhamsted gang involved in stealing Post Office mailbags.

The gang, which included three brothers, were given sentences ranging from three months to five years when they appeared at Herts Quarter Sessions at St Albans on Friday.

The court heard that over a period of five months, nine mailbags containing property valued at over £680, were stolen. 'D' rings from the tops of the bags were recovered from an incinerator at Berkhamsted station.

Police discovered 'an enormous amount' of the stolen property stowed away in the loft of the Gossoms End home of the brothers. Burnt remains of stolen clothing were found in the garden.

CHEQUE

The chain of events which led to the arrest started at a bank in St Albans when one of the gang tried to cash a cheque for £10.

A clerk at the Midland Bank spotted that the signature on the cheque had been printed with a rubber stamp. She told the assistant manager about it and the Police were informed.

Statements by the gang admitting involvement in the crime were read to the court and all five were given jail sentences.

The full newspaper report included defence statements. They spoke of family splits, living rough and a broken engagement

I looked at the finished report with a ludicrous sense of achievement: I had at last covered a court case. It may not have been a brilliant piece of reporting but it was an accurate representation of what occurred in court. I had this notion that until you had covered a court case you had not properly earned your reporter's stripes; I've no idea why.

It was the one and only time I entered a court to report for the Gazette.

Chapter 37

Jane's daily appearance in the Berko office was a mixed blessing. There she was, always looking great, working diligently on the boring routine reports that are the lifeblood of a local paper: monthly meetings of the WI with their inevitable potato print competitions; endless weddings where the vital ingredients of brides and bridesmaids' dress descriptions, honeymoon destination and future place of residence had to be faithfully recorded; and conversion of parish council minutes into readable English. The downside was that I was unable, during office hours, to do any up of the chatting nature knowing that every word and move was being closely scrutinised by Janet and Mel. All I could do was occasionally stare at her and hope that nobody would notice. I was also unsure as to whether or not she had a current boyfriend: I was out of the Hemel gossip loop and daren't mention the matter for fear of ridicule.

However, a genuine opportunity to get to know her better - and at firm's expense - occurred when sporting icon Henry Cooper came to town.

Janet was opening the post as usual and in amongst the ads, readers letters and scribblings of various club secretaries was an invitation to a charity ball.

"You'll probably want to cover this," she said as she tossed the invitation my direction.

"Oh, great....another Saturday job," I said as I saw the event date in heavy bold type.

"Read the rest of it," Janet commanded.

"Blooooody hell....Henry Cooper!"

"Thought that might make you pay attention."

Like millions of Brits, I loved Henry Cooper. He epitomised all the best elements of a genuine sportsman. Not only was he an immensely skilled boxer but he was always as gracious in victory as he was on the rare occasions he lost a bout. He had thrilled the nation with many a spectacular performance and in particular in 1963 when he dumped the then Cassius Clay on his arse with a pearler of a left hook that would have had the up and coming world champ counted out if the bell had not rung for the end of the round. And now he was coming to Berkhamsted.

"Yes. I think I might just do that one."

"The invitation is for you and a guest," said Janet looking towards Jane, "so no prizes for guessing who you might be taking."

"For two is it? I hadn't noticed."

"Liar."

I ignored her jibe.

"Well?"

"Well what?"

"Well, who are you going to ask to go with you?"

"I haven't decided. Anyway, it's not compulsory to go with a guest...I'll probably go on my own."

As soon as Janet left for the day and Mel popped out to get an Echo I cleared my throat and stood up.

"Er...Jane. By any chance are you free on Saturday night to go to a ball with...er..with me?"

"Yes. That'll be lovely."

"I mean...you don't have to. It's only a ....er...only a..."

"Only a what?"

"I dunno...em..a work thing. That's right. It might not be your cup of tea."

I could sense that my mouth, already full of one foot was preparing itself for a second helping as I raced at breakneck speed to snatch defeat from the jaws of victory.

"Well, I'm not doing anything on Saturday evening. And didn't I hear you say that Henry Cooper will be attending?"

"Yes. That's right. Do you like Henry Cooper?"

"I haven't really given the subject much thought," she said with a grin. "But you clearly like him."

"Like him....I'll say I like him. So you'll come then?"

"Yes, I've already accepted your invitation."

"Would you like me to collect you...say sevenish?"

"That'll be great. Right. I'm off. See you tomorrow."

Over the next few days I desperately tried to adopt an insouciant bearing in the office, pretending not to hear loaded remarks from Janet and Mel about my Saturday night companion.

The ball was being held at Ashlyns school to raise money for what was then known as the Spastics Games, an event established for sports men and women with cerebral palsy. Henry Cooper was renowned for his charity work and his appearance would help ensure a bucket load of cash would be raised.

On the Saturday afternoon I cleared out the rubbish from my Morris Minor and thought about washing the car. I couldn't be bothered so concentrated instead on cleaning the bird crap off the windscreen. I turned up at Jane's house on time and we drove back to Berkhamsted and up the school drive to the main car park. The school hall was packed with nearly 300 (we rarely stated actual figures in copy; it was always 'more than' or 'nearly' a round number).

Jane and I were allocated a table with a group of local worthies with whom we made small talk as the Nat Temple Band played and illusionist Robert Harben entertained guests with his mystifying tricks. There was a lucky draw which included a basket of fruit which was won by Henry whose outside business interests included...a green grocer's shop.

Henry, dressed in a DJ with white shirt and bow tie was seated at a table with his Italian wife Albina and the organisers of the ball.

I have to admit to being star struck and I desperately wanted to speak to Henry who, of course, was constantly surrounded by people who also wanted a chat. I hopped around at the edge of one such group for what seemed like ages before blurting out: "Er..Mr Cooper. I'm Paul Barnes from the Berkhamsted Gazette.....can we have a photo please?"

Simon snapped the British heavyweight champion with three very attractive can-can dancers - Valerie Hine from Little Chalfont, Susan Barrett of Chesham Bois and Jo Hanika from Chesham.

I hovered around as Simon went to work and when he finished I stammered out a question about the evening to which he politely replied that he had "thoroughly enjoyed" the occasion. After that scoop I nervously went into proper reporter mode by asking him a boxing related question. Henry had twice won the European heavyweight title and there was speculation about his trying to win it a third time.

"Mr Cooper....

"It's Henry, Paul."

He called me Paul. He wants me to call him Henry. Can life get any better?

"Oh, yes, er Henry, are you going to fight Urtain for the European title?"

Jose Manuel Urtain was the current EBU champion and the two had never met in the ring. Urtain at that time appeared indestructible having won his first thirty bouts by knockout; his only defeat being a disqualification. He would be a fearsome opponent for Henry Cooper whose career was littered with stopped contests due to his propensity to cut easily.

"Oh, that's just paper talk," he replied before adding: "No disrespect to you, Paul."

This was Henry Cooper OBE, British and Commonwealth Heavyweight champion and former European Heavyweight title-holder apologising to me for any offence he may have caused by referring to "paper talk". No wonder I was star struck.

I was on the verge of asking for his autograph before realising that I might be considered unprofessional by the great man.

I wandered back to the table where Jane was nursing a nearly finished snowball.

"What did he say?" she asked.

"He called me Paul. Twice."

"Are you going to quote him on that?"

"Uhh....? Oh, sorry. Yes I've got a quote about the do. Would you like another drink?"

"Snowball, please."

As I drifted across to the bar I wondered if the night could get any better. Jane was not only stunning but also great company and mixed well with the other guests. I started to imagine how I would approach the question of going out on a proper date. I made up my mind to ask her when I dropped her off at her house in Hillfield Road. As we neared Hemel she suddenly said: "Can you keep a secret?"

Wayhey...another positive sign of a blossoming romance.

"Of course. What is it?"

"Promise you won't tell anyone in the Hemel or Berko offices. Well not yet."

"I promise."

"Well. I've got a new job. I'm leaving the Gazette."

"Wow. Where are you off to? Don't tell me you're going to the Echo."

"No. I've landed a feature writer's job on Rave. It's a monthly magazine aimed at the teenage market."

My heart sunk. I felt awful.

"Oh....that's...that's great. Well done."

"Yes. I went for an interview last week and they rang me at home this evening.."

"At home.....? Blimey, they must be keen. When do you start?"

"As soon as possible. Subject to Ronnie not playing silly buggers about notice periods, I can start inside a couple of weeks."

"Bloody hell...that's quick."

"I just had to tell someone...I'm so excited."

"Where is Rave based."

"London."

"I suppose you'll be commuting. That'll be a bit pricey."

"No. I'm going to live in London...in Kentish Town with my sister."

"When are you going to tell Ronnie? And why have you told me?"

"I'll be telling Ronnie on Monday, but I wanted you to know as soon as possible so you've got a bit of time to get somebody in to replace me."

"Oh...thanks. That's very good of you seeing as it's Saturday night. Sorry, that didn't quite come out right. What I meant to say is that I can't see me getting a replacement before you leave."

"Oh no...I suppose not. Sorry."

"No...no, you've got nothing to apologise for. It sounds like a great opportunity. Only wish I...."

I didn't feel it was the right time to add the words "...was going with you".

"What do you wish?"

"Er...wish I could get another job."

This was true. But I'm not sure I properly disguised my disappointment at her news. London....London! Now I'll never see her. By the time we got to her house all thoughts of asking her out had disappeared. What would be the point? Even if she said yes, it would not go anywhere.

"Do you want to come in for a coffee, Paul?"

Twenty minutes ago I'd have taken up her invitation like a shot but now all I wanted to do was go home and drown my sorrows and look for a cat to kick.

"No thanks, Jane. See you Monday. Bye."

"Oh...right, okay. Yes. See you then. Thanks for...."

I didn't hear the rest of the sentence as I'd already pulled away from the kerb and was driving back down the road. What a bloody day. One minute in seventh heaven, the next experiencing fate's pooh land squarely on my head.

Chapter 38

It wasn't often that we were able to include the names of Miss Barbara Russell, Headmistress of Berkhamsted School for Girls, and the famous female 'plane hijacker Leila Khaled in the same story. It happened in the Gazette September 18, 1970.

And the story helped save my personal journalistic integrity; never have I been more grateful for a 'plane hijacking.

It had been a very slow news week locally with bugger-all going on. Normally by Tuesday I had a good idea of what was going to be front page lead; there could be a strong up-coming agenda item at a council meeting or there'd been yet another fatal on the A41.

But there was nothing.

I sifted through the day's post in the hope that someone had sent in something that could be turned into a lead story. Nothing. Tried 'phoning the fire and ambulance services. Nothing. Cops?...a fat zero. Even our loquacious local vicar, not normally slow in coming forward with something controversial in his sermon, was no help. In fairness, he was away on holiday.

'Oh, this is bloody ridiculous. I've been here four effing years and this is the first time I can remember not having anything strong enough for the front lead.'

In desperation, I 'phoned Hemel. It was the last thing I wanted to do. To explain to that bunch of piss-takers that I hadn't got anything for the front page lead was, to my mind, a huge admission of failure.

Fortunately it was Wendy who took my call.

"Oh, hi Wendy. It's Paul. Just er wondering if there's any court stuff with a Berko angle that you've got for this week's paper?"

Hemel reporters for some historical reason always covered quarter sessions in St Albans, and the magistrates courts in Hemel and Berkhamsted.

"They haven't really got going after the summer break, so, no, sorry Paul. Do you need to fill a gap?"

I decided to brazen it out.

"Nah...I'm ok."

"You sure?"

"Yes. Got plenty of stuff. Cheers, then."

"Cheerio, Paul."

I put the 'phone down and strode out of the office and shouted loudly in confines of the overgrown weed strewn patch that passed as the garden: "Bollocks, bollocks and even more bollocks!"

I was going to have to create something: make up a story. I couldn't think of any other solution. What could I do that wouldn't do any real harm? It would have to be something feasible that nobody would suss. Something that nobody would think of checking.

I wandered down to the canal pondering various scenarios that didn't actually involve anyone. As I sat staring at the water it came to me. What if I jumped in the water and rescued myself? No, that wouldn't work. I could pretend that I'd fallen in and that a passer-by had helped me out. And I could report that I'd been rescued by someone who wished to remain anonymous. That could work.

I looked at the murky water with the ducks swimming towards me in the hope of food. I just couldn't do it. I didn't want to get wet and cold. There had to be a better way.

'Wet and cold. That's it. Well not wet exactly, but damp certainly.'

I rushed back to the office. My plan was to invent a dampness problem in some local council houses. My source would, of course, have to be anonymous. The Council could check it out and find there was no damp problem. And, Hey Presto, front page lead with big bold 48 point u&l heading over five: "Council denies housing damp problem".

I rang the council offices feeling nervous, and very very guilty. "Is Mr Oates, the housing manager available?"

"Who is it, please?"

"Paul Barnes. Gazette."

"Hold on."

"Hello Paul. What can I do for you?"

Oh, shit he's such a good bloke. But the die was cast.

"Oh, er, sorry to bother you Mr Oates, but we've had a report of damp in some council houses."

"Really? Where?"

"Um ..it's um..Durrants Road, Gossoms End."

"What numbers?"

Oh, Christ. I hadn't thought of *which* houses.

"Oh, the caller didn't give me their name or where they lived. Just said it was houses in Durrants Road. I'm just checking it out."

"I'll look into it and call you back."

He was as good as his word. "We've had absolutely no reports of damp in houses in Durrants Road. And to be quite frank I'd have been very surprised if there was a problem as we only completed a maintenance check of them all a few weeks ago."

"Oh, right, thanks. I'll make that clear in the story."

"Not much of a story, is it though? But I suppose you've got a job to do."

Whether he smelt a rat, I couldn't tell. But I had a story. I would quote him in full about there having been a maintenance check and that his department had received no complaints of damp from anyone in the road. I could even dress it up as a mysterious damp problem. 'Yes, even better'. I started typing furiously to get the story done and hoped that my conscience could bear the strain of the ridiculous subterfuge that had been used to get a crap story.

I knocked out eight pars....barely enough, but padded it out with invented quotes from the anonymous tenant.

I stared at my work. The words of Les Oates came back to me, 'not much of a story...but I suppose you've got a job to do'.

"Shit, shit, shit." I ripped up the copy, screwed it into a ball and threw it in the bin.

"Problem?"

"Oh, nothing important Mel.....just haven't got anything for front page lead."

"What? Not even a council story?"

"Sod all."

"Something'll turn up," he offered unhelpfully. "Let's go for a pint."

"How can I go for a pint? I've got to get something. And I've got very little time to do it."

"Fretting about it ain't going to help. C'mon. It's nearly lunchtime. You've got the whole afternoon to worry about getting a story. I'll let you have one of mine if you like."

He had that irritating piss-taking gleam in his eye. A Tring piece as a Berko lead? Never.

"Oh, what the hell."

"You want one of my stories?"

"No, you pillock...a pint."

We slipped down to the Black Horse.

"Hi boys...the usual?"

The cheery greeting came from Reg Watts, the affable landlord and occasional story informant.

"Yes please, Reg."

He set about pouring two light and bitters as I stood at the bar.

"That was some tale about those girls from the girls' school, wasn't it?"

"Eh ? What girls?"

"You, know...the ones on that plane."

"What plane?".

"You know...the one in the desert."

"Desert? Plane?"

"You know......that'll be six and tuppence."

"Reg...what the hell are you on about?"

"Oh, sorry Paul...I thought you would have known."

By now I was beside myself with irritation.

"Known what, Reg?"

"Well, I got the usual milk delivery this morning from, Norman. You know Norman."

"No I don't bloody know Norman. What are you on about?"

"Well, Norman had delivered milk up to the school and he heard from the caretaker that four of the girls from the school were on that hijacked plane. Sorry, I thought you would have known."

"Reg. You're a life-saver. I could kiss you...or at least give you a manly hand-shake. Come on Mel, drink up. I've got a front page lead to write."

Mel, disappointed that he was having to rush his lunch, nevertheless did as requested and we hurried back to the office, burping loudly.

The plane to which Reg was referring, a BOAC VC10 with 105 passengers and nine crew, was one of five aircraft to be hijacked by the Popular Front for the Liberation of Palestine within a few days of each other. Four of the planes had been heading for the USA and the fifth, the VC10, to London Heathrow. They landed at Dawson's Field in Jordan, a former RAF base renamed 'Revolution Airfield' by the PFLP, where the girls along with other passengers were held hostage for several days

When I got back I managed to get through to the school and spoke to the Headmistress, Miss Russell who was reluctant at first to talk about the girls but admitted that there were four of our girls, two pairs of sisters, on the plane and no, they had not yet returned to school. She also mentioned that she had led the school in prayers for the girls' safe return. I mouthed a curse that we had not learnt about the girls until that day; it would have saved a lot of personal anguish about story inventing. After some discussion I was able to locate where two of the sisters were staying in Berkhamsted.

I beetled round to the North Road home of Mrs Ruth Warren, the girls' school term guardian. The sisters and their parents had only recently arrived and I had very little time to conduct the interview and get the story written. Simon arrived to take the pictures and his terrific shot of the girls being embraced by Mum and Dad graced five columns of the September18 front page.

The girls' story proved to be one of the very best published by the Gazette during my time with the paper.

Under a 60pt Tempo Bold caps eight-column streamer heading

SCHOOLGIRLS' ORDEAL ON HIJACK JET

the opening paragraph in bold across three read:

"After spending four days under the threat of their hijacked B.O.A.C. VC10 being blown to pieces with the passengers on board, Margaret and Rhoda McGowan of Berkhamsted School for Girls tell of their harrowing and sometimes terrifying experiences. Their story of how they were treated by the Palestinian guerrillas is tinged with both humour and excitement. The incredibility of the whole fantastic situation may be emphasised by the fact that the girls managed to obtain autographs of those who were threatening their lives."

The girls had been visiting their parents during the school summer holiday and were returning to the UK on September 9 when their plane was hijacked. The guerrillas told their hostages that they wanted the release of Leilah Khaled who had been captured during a failed attempt to hijack an El Al flight from Amsterdam to New York earlier in the month.

The two girls were travelling in the first class section of the plane. In the seat in front of them sat one of the hijackers.

About two hours into the flight - half way between Bahrain and Beirut - the hijacker stood up and ushered the cabin crew out.

Margaret said: "He ordered us into the economy class with a gun at our backs.

Over the plane's loudspeaker came the words "this is a PFLP hijack".

The plane landed at Beirut where more PFLP personnel were picked up. It then flew on to the desert landing strip destination.

The girls told of being confined within the baking temperatures of the plane and of getting mixed messages about their fate.

"Someone said that the hijackers would blow us up and themselves too,
but then other people on board said they wouldn't," said Margaret.

The hostages were held for nearly four days.

"It was hot and sticky," said Rhoda, "but not as hot as I thought it would be. We had heard the temperature would be 120 degrees."

Food was shared by hijackers who gave out Lebanese bread, cheese and tomatoes.

Amongst the five hijackers guarding their plane were thirteen and fifteen-year-old boys, both with guns, who spoke a little English.

All the passengers were "very calm" fourteen-year-old Margaret said: "No-one got upset except a little Indian boy who cried all the first night. The guerrillas were very nice and we were allowed to do very much what we liked. We were let out of the plane for 20 minutes altogether....we wandered about near the plane, in the shade."

The hostages spent some time singing pop songs and made up their own version of 'Yellow Submarine' which included the line 'we all live in a blue and white machine' (the colours of the VC10).

The guerrillas tried to teach the girls how to say the Popular Front for the Liberation of Palestine in Arabic. They also handed out leaflets to the passengers that explained the cause of the PFLP.

It was on these leaflets that the McGowan sisters collected some forty autographs of hijackers, passengers and crew. These autographed leaflets were later temporarily taken by airline officials 'for security reasons'.

Their eventual release, gained after the British government agreed to free Leilah Khaled's freedom from custody in London, coincided with Rhoda's thirteenth birthday. The occasion was made even more memorable by her dad Ron, himself an airline pilot, radioing through a birthday message to his daughter's homebound plane and the passengers singing 'Happy Birthday' as she was presented with a iced Dundee cake with straws for candles by the captain and crew.

Back in Berkhamsted, when asked how she felt at hearing news of the girls' release and arrival at Heathrow, their mother Mrs Margaret McGowan just sighed: "Relief."

She also commented that the guerrillas "must have remarkable character to be able to point a gun at someone and be thought very nice".

The other Berkhamsted Girls Schoolgirl hostages were fifteen-year-old Juliet Garman and her thirteen year-old sister Carolyn.

In a perfect study of schoolmarmish understatement, Miss Russell said of the girls' safe return: "We are naturally very pleased. They have had a very tiring experience and I should think they would want to merge back into the school scene. There won't be any fuss."

She added that the girls would have to make up "an important week's school work".

Chapter 39

After such a powerful story of the girls on the hijacked jet I was not expecting another attention-grabbing story for the following week's paper. But I needn't have worried; I got another belter thanks in part to Mum. Being Bursar at Ashlyns School, Mum knew just about everything that was going on and was a good news contact, as well as a provider of emergency funding for car repairs.

"The Head's banned cross country runs for the foreseeable future," she told me over a post-work cuppa. "There was some kind of shooting incident."

"Bloody hell, Ma. What kind of shooting?"

"I'm not sure, Love. But I asked Mr Babington if it would be ok if I told you about it. And would it be okay if you spoke to him in the morning?"

"That's terrific, Ma. Many tahs."

The following day I got in touch with the Head, John Babington. Unlike the somewhat terse responses to questions I got from the Girls School Head Miss Russell, he readily agreed to chat. He explained that, on police advice, he had suspended the runs following an incident the previous week. He had announced the suspension at the school assembly.

He also granted my request to speak to some of the fifth year boys who were witness to the shooting in woods just off Swing Gate Lane. They were on the last stage of their run on a track leading towards Ashlyns Hall when they first saw a man with a rifle.

Under the 72pt Tempo bold u&l four deck centred over three column

Cross Country Runs Banned After Shooting Incident

the Gazette report opened across three columns in 14pt bold:

HEADMASTER OF ASHLYNS SCHOOL Mr. J. H. Babington has banned school cross-country runs until further notice following last week's incident when a man with a rifle "aimed shots" at boys in woods just off Swing Gate Lane.

Mr. Babington made the announcement to the school assembly on Wednesday morning. He told the "Gazette" later that he wanted more information on the incident before making another decision on the matter. It is understood that the police who are making enquiries into the incident advised the school to suspend cross-country runs.

It was on Wednesday last week as about a dozen fifth year boys were on the last stage of their cross-country run that a man with a gun fired shots. The boys were on a track leading towards Ashlyns Hall; a route normally used by the school for cross-country runs.

One of the boys, Philip Nickolay (15) who lives at 50 Orchard Avenue, took up the story. "We heard a shot and turned round and saw a man come out of the bushes behind us. He had a gun and seemed to take aim and we dodged into the bushes at the side of the track. I heard him shoot.

"We came out of the bushes and he was just standing there with the gun at his side about 100 yards away. We carried on running and reported the incident to Mr Hughes, the games master, when we got back to school. We were later seen by the police."

Philip said the man was between 20 and 40 and was wearing a light coloured pullover.

His mother, Mrs Alys Nickolay said: "I would not be happy about the boys going on the run again unless there was somebody around to safeguard them. I think the police ought to be watching out up there. The person with the rifle might be some crank individual who is anti kids."

Two other boys who were on the run, Robert Benbridge of 9 Orchard Avenue and Kim Humphries of 49 South Park Gardens, both 15, said that they actually heard the bullets ricochet of trees and branches.

They said that the man was about 75 yards away and that they had stopped running and were facing him before he fired the first shot. "I think he was aiming above our heads and I heard the bullet hit a tree," explained Robert.

The boys ducked into bushes and waited there for about 30 seconds. "We looked out and the man had moved out into the track. He took aim again," said Kim, who added that he heard a bullet "rattle through the branches."

They then ran off. "We didn't want to hang around," commented Robert.

Gary Davidson (15) was about 300 yards behind the main group running on his own when the incident occurred.

Gary, who lives at 15 Clarence Road, said: "I did not see the man aiming at the others. When I ran past him he was just shooting in the trees. I did not know anything had happened until I caught up with the other boys."

According to Gary, the man was of medium height, about 30 with darkish coloured hair. The rifle looked to him to be a high powered air rifle.

The story shared a front page full of very strong news stories including a court case involving two drug using brothers who were caught in possession of cannabis and who had stolen tablets. They were apprehended after a baby in a neighbouring house had been reported to have swallowed three tranquiliser capsules.

There was also news of an inquest into the deaths of two people on the A41 and a £2000 smash and grab raid at a local jewellers.

Chapter 40

Although not usually a relater of unusual stories, the Gazette was able to produce some cracking tales without always realising their significance. Take for example the day Cliff came to Northchurch, a small but attractive adjunct to the town which is bisected by the old A41.

It was October 1970 and I was spending more and more time applying for jobs away from Berko. I was getting fed up with the never-ending stream of stock diary stories we were doing such as pensioners' mystery tours, gymkhanas and school sports days with the same old faces taking part in the same old events. And there was the constant battle to avoid resorting to 'blooming' in the headlines when describing a local flower and produce show. I was also more than a bit peeved with my miserable weekly imbursement which was destined to pay off the weekly car repair bills. I'd tried tackling Tommy about my pay, complaining that with Harry's regular alcohol-related leaves of absence I was not only reporting and subbing, I was laying out and editing the Berko pages, so an increase in pay would not come amiss.

"Yeth Mither Barnth, I recognith that you have been working hard and I promith to amend your Chrithmuth bonuth to reflect all that you have done."

Instead of the usual £2 10s, Tommy awarded me £4.

Because of the constant pressure and build up of work I found myself looking for excuses to get out of doing stories.

Lizzie Blackwood, a trainee reporter, had recently joined the paper and was sent to work at Berkhamsted. I was nominally in charge of her development but it was difficult to properly train her as I was spending most of my time chasing my tail trying to meet deadlines.

I was looking through some mail that Janet had left on my desk when I saw an invitation from Northchurch Baptist Church for Sunday 11th October. It stated that Cliff Richard would be attending the church to talk about his faith and the evils of drug abuse.

Instead of welcoming what was obviously going to be a page lead I just whined.

"Sod it, sod it," I groaned out loud. "Another bloody Sunday job for muggins."

"What is it?" asked Lizzie.

"It's Cliff Richard coming to Northchurch on Sunday week."

"Wow....that's fantastic! Cliff? Please let me do it. Pleeease."

"Don't tell me you actually like Cliff."

By 1970, like most of the Beatles and Stones generation, I had adopted a pretentious disdain for the saintly crooner and his bland renditions of bland songs. But he was a big name and it would be a big local story.

"I absolutely love him. I know all his songs. I do a particularly good version of 'Congratulations'. Would you like to hear it?"

"No I bloody would not. It's a crap song."

"If you don't let me do the job, I'll sing it over and over and over again."

Christ, I thought. She means it. She's happy to work on a Sunday and she likes Cliff.

"Make us a coffee, and I'll think about it. I mean this is an important story and I should really be doing it. You're still a trainee and.....no....don't you dare....I'm warning you!"

It was too late.

"Dum de dum de dum dum...boom boom boom boom....congratulations, and jubilations..."

"Stop, stop. For Christ's sake, Lizzie stop. You can do the job."

"Thank you boss."

She only called me boss when she was taking the piss. But what a result. I get out of working on Sunday.

As it happened, Cliff's appearance at the church was just three days before his thirtieth birthday and Billy Baxendale had a shot of him holding a card given to him by people at the church. It was a good picture so I stuck it on the front page over five columns.

"Hmm what possible headline could I come up with to grace this shot.....Oh bloody no...surely not....it has to be...'Conbloodygratulations'."

"I'd leave the 'bloody' out of that if I were you," smirked Janet."Cliff would not approve."

So the front page had the picture of Cliff and three paragraphs about it being his birthday:

"Showing off a birthday card presented to him for his thirtieth birthday on Wednesday is pop singer Cliff Richard who spoke to the congregation of Northchurch Baptist Church on Sunday.

Because so many people wanted to have the opportunity to speak to Cliff at the gathering after the service, only those who were over 14 and under 30 were admitted. They heard him speak on the subjects of drugs, war, show business, as well as his own religious beliefs.

During both the service and the meeting afterwards, Cliff sang a number of gospel songs and a poem 'Indifference' for which he wrote the tune. For a full report on the pop star's visit to the church, see page five."

Lizzie had beamed at me as she triumphantly handed over the copy; and she had done a fine job.

"Did he REALLY say that?"

"Look, I might be a trainee but I know what I heard and my shorthand's pretty good. He said it alright."

"But it's....it's...well...bollocks."

"I'm telling you that's what he said."

"Oh well....you were right to make it your intro. This is certainly going to shake up a few people."

Thus followed one of my most memorable headlines, in 36point Roman bold caps across two columns:

**ONLY JESUS
COULD HAVE
SAFELY
TAKEN L.S.D
-CLIFF**

The story, despite some haphazard subbing, certainly did not let the headline down:

Jesus Christ was the only person who could have taken L.S.D safely, because he was the only one with a pure mind, pop singer Cliff Richard told 200 youngsters at Northchurch Baptist Church on Sunday.

Cliff was speaking at a meeting in the Church Hall after the evening church service at which he had answered questions on his religious beliefs.

He told youngsters that L.S.D brought out the bad things in the takers' minds. "Dabbling with drugs is dangerous, forget it," he continued. "Drugs are a cheap way out, like suicide."

With Cliff was Bill Latham, Education Officer of the T.E.A.R Fund - the Evangelical Alliance Relief Fund - a Christian organisation which collects money to help famine stricken countries.

The Baptist Church Secretary Mr Alan Dyer knew Bill Latham when they were both members of the Crusaders organisation. "It was through personal contact Cliff and Bill came here," said Mr Dyer.

Instead of preaching a sermon.....Cliff was questioned by Bill about his religious beliefs.

Cliff said he had been the subject of much criticism since he first became a Christian six years ago.

"MY JOB"

"I'm asked why I'm not a missionary out in Africa," he said. "But show business is my job, (while) slap bang in the middle of my life

is Christianity. To me, the most natural thing in the world is my belief in Jesus."

To some people their religious beliefs are a personal thing which they don't talk about, Bill said. How did Cliff feel about the amount of publicity he got?

But Cliff pointed out that if Christians did not talk to other people about Jesus, how could Christianity spread?

"I spent three years asking questions about Christianity," said Cliff. "If everyone had kept quiet, how would I have found out about it?"

Because he was famous, Cliff said, he naturally drew crowds and was able to speak to them about Christianity.

He asked the Northchurch congregation how many of them would have gone to church if he had not been speaking. People came to meetings to see the pop star, but once they were there, they would have to listen to his views on Christianity.

What did Cliff feel about the ridicule Christians were often subjected to?

"It takes a far stronger person to stand up against jeering and say 'I don't care' than it does to laugh at someone." He said that people who once laughed at him because of his beliefs now respected his views and respected him for keeping to them.

"If you are a Christian you are a non-conformist, one of a minority group. People in some countries are still being persecuted for their Christian beliefs and even go to jail for them.
"Christianity has the God power; it now needs the man power," Cliff added.

After the service Cliff answered more questions, this time by the young people.

War was the first topic Cliff was asked about.

He said that many young people asked:"If God is so good why doesn't he do something about the Vietnam war?"

"God said love thy enemy," Cliff continued. "If we did everything God said, there would never be any more wars. It is as childishly simple as that."

Would he fight in any future war? Cliff replied: "If I felt strongly against Communism, then it would be my duty and right to fight against it. But I wouldn't fight with the army because for one thing they are not fighting for God.

"I would be a conscientious objector to conscription," he added.

RELY ON GOD

Cliff thought people should rely on God more to help them solve their problems.

He was asked if his Christian principles affected the type of jokes told in shows etc. There had been a few sketches presented to him to use in his TV series which had been rejected because of their suggestiveness, but Cliff said the rejections had been the decision of all people involved in the production.

There had also been songs which he would have liked to have sung but which were discarded for the same reason.
The collection during the service will be donated entirely to the T.E.A.R fund.

I awaited, with keen anticipation, the reaction to this bombshell of a story: how would the good folk of Berkhamsted and district respond?. Was there a flood of correspondence? Was there buggery. Not one solitary sodding letter.

The main missive in the following week's paper was from a John Dunbavand of Darrs Lane, Shootersway complaining about Berkhamsted Urban District Council's plans to site a rubbish tip at the old brickworks in Shootersway.

 Ah the power of the press.

Chapter 41

Whilst we would never profess to be a campaigning paper, we nevertheless managed to shine the occasional light on a local problem that needed solving. One such issue involved what we termed in 1970 'gipsy tent dwellers'.

Their plight came to our attention in March when we followed up a piece in the Echo about the extended Parker family who were living in four tents in the woods at Brickhill Green just off the A416 Chesham Road between Berkhamsted and Ashley Green.

There were fifteen family members including 52-year-old Beatrice, a mother of six, four of whom she had borne under canvas. Her husband, Lucas also known as Levi, earned cash as a knife and shears grinder. They had applied to Berkhamsted Urban District Council to be included on its housing list.

In what a local district councillor Diana Allen called "a clear case of harassment", in April they were moved on by the police and pitched up at Two Ponds Lane on the outskirts of Northchurch. After a two-week stay we reported in the Gazette of May 8 that they intended moving back to Brickhill Green "because it is nearer the town centre (of Berkhamsted)". We also recorded that 14-year-old son Peter (Isaac) Parker had started at Ashlyns School and had learnt how to write his own name, thus becoming "the first Parker to accomplish this feat".

The Parkers would feature in the paper on several occasions over the next few weeks.

Gazette May 29, 1970....The Parkers refuse to leave Brickhill Green after police tell them to go.

Gazette June 12, 1970....Berkhamsted Urban District Council to hold a special meeting in July to discuss housing for gipsy families.

Gazette July 10, 1970....Lead story on front page was the Housing Committee discussion off the Parkers' application. Housing Manager told members that Lucas Parker was now working for the council as a grass cutter.

Councillor Geoffrey Lancashire said: "By this they qualify and should be put on the list. We should not be concerned whether applicants are black, white, yellow, gipsies, accountants, teachers or local government workers; they are human beings."

Before the family moved into a council house they should spend some time at a rehabilitation centre, urged Councillor Jack Rickard.

"They have never lived in a house," he said. "Therefore the county council should take these people into a hostel."

But Councillor Ian Miller asked why the gipsies should have to go "through this cleansing process you call rehabilitation. Perhaps it is we who are living abnormally."

The council should have no special policy concerning gipsies, he said, ie if they work or live in the town, then their names should be put down if they qualify for inclusion on the list.

"But if someone pitches a tent within U.D.C. boundaries that cannot be construed as being resident," he added.

The Committee recommended that the Parkers' application for inclusion on the housing list be approved and submitted to the full council for final approval.

It was previously reported that the Parkers' application to Berkhamsted Rural District Council for inclusion on its housing list had been approved.

Gazette August 14, 1970....Parker children Peter and Margaret to get home tutor.

Gazette December 4, 1970....Beatrice and Lucas and four of their children, move into 12 Provident Place, Berkhamsted, a Hertfordshire County Council-owned property designated for use by homeless families.

Mrs Parker said: "It's very nice and a lot better than the last place."

Chapter 42

By the autumn of 1970 I was really getting fed up with life on the Gazette. Jane was reputedly thoroughly enjoying life on Rave magazine where she was interviewing pop stars and writing teen features and I was missing her although we'd never been on a proper date. I was even fighting feelings of jealousy at the thought that she might be getting off with the bass player of Herman's Hermits or Radio 1 deejay Tony Blackburn who she had, as part of her duties, taken to the cinema to get a review of a new film.

"Tony Blackburn! Bloody ridiculous being jealous of Tony Blackburn," I muttered."Get a grip Paul."

"Did you say something?" Mel looked up from reading the UK Press Gazette.

"No....nothing. Any jobs in there?"

"A couple. Why? You wanna leave as well?"

"I wouldn't say no if the right job cropped up."

"Let me see...hmm. Can't see any that might appeal. None with the words miserable bastard wanted..." He chuckled and Janet hooted with laughter at his witty reference to my sullen demeanour.

I frowned at their pleasure in my discomfort.

"Yeah. Very bloody funny."

"Well. You've been a right misery guts since a certain lady left the paper. Why the hell didn't you ask her out? Everyone knows that you fancied her like mad," said Mel.

'Everyone knows....everyone knows. How the bloody hell can everyone know that I fancy her? I've kept my feelings to myself'.

"Dunno what you're on about. I'm just getting a bit fed up with this place, that's all. Alright?"

"If you say so."

"Yes....I do say so."

Mel then did that hugely embarrassing thing of imitating some camp comedian with a high-pitched effeminate 'ooooohhh' as I snatched the magazine from his desk. Christ, was my fancying Jane like the clappers that obvious?

I scanned the jobs. I'd already had a pop at joining the enemy - The Echo - and all they'd offered was an advertising features writer/sub job. The money was better but my stupid pride would not allow me to take what I thought was an inferior position. The thought of having to write puffs about local garages or suppliers of stationery made me cringe.

There were quite a few local paper jobs....but I wasn't really interested in doing what I did on the Gazette in another part of the country. I wanted to make the step to an evening or, if possible, a national daily. Then I spotted a PR job with the London Borough of Hackney. The ad job description stressed journalistic skills and the opportunity to help promote the work of the council in a racially mixed community. And then I saw the salary. It was twice what I was being paid by the Gazette.

I immediately set about replenishing my CV and by the end of the day my application for the job was winging its way to the Council's PR office in Mare Street, E8.

A couple of weeks later I was more than a bit delighted to get an invitation to an interview. To cut a long story short I was interviewed in the Hackney Town Hall by the Council's PRO and a top administration guy who offered me the job; there and then...no messing about. I immediately said yes and agreed to start the first week of January 1971 I floated out of the building on all the clouds leading up to number nine. This called for a celebration. However, it was three in the afternoon and the boozers were shut.

"I know what I'm going to do; something I should have done years ago," I said to nobody in particular upstairs on the number 30 back to Euston. I hopped off the bus at King's Cross and made my way down King's Cross Road towards Clerkenwell. As I got closer to Farringdon House in Farringdon my heart began to beat more than a tad quicker. I entered the building and viewed the display board that included the names of several magazines including Honey, Petticoat, Mirabel, Fab 208 and, on one of the upper floors, Rave.

"Can I help you...?". I turned to respond to the receptionist.

"Oh, yes, um....I've, er, got an appointment with someone on Rave."

"Name?"

"Oh, yes...it's Paul Barnes."

"Hold on." She reached for the 'phone and dialled a number."Hi. Got someone here who wants to speak to a Paul Barnes."

I started gesticulating as she continued her conversation.

"Right. Fine. Tah. I will tell him."

She turned to gaze at my blushing face. "They're sending someone down. Take a seat."

"But...I...um. I'm Paul....I mean I want to speak to....".

But by now the woman was answering an incoming call and had clearly lost interest in who I was. As far as she was concerned I had been quickly and efficiently dealt with. I did as I was told and wondered who the hell would be coming to see me. Somebody in Security perhaps to escort me from the premises? I picked up a copy of one of the magazines on the table in front of me and pretended to read it. I could feel the sweat gathering under my arms. I gave my armpits a quick sniff whilst the receptionist wasn't looking.

And then she was there, walking through the opening door of the lift. Jane. Looking absolutely fantastic. She crossed the reception area to where I was seated with an expression of puzzlement and delight.

"Hi Paul. Just by chance it was me who took the call just now. l realised it was you here. What a nice surprise."

I stood up.

"I just wanted to come and see you. And tell you..tell you...."

She took my hand and kissed me.

On the lips.

"It's wonderful to see you. Let's go for a coffee."

The End

Acknowledgements

I am not going to fall into the trap of attempting to name every individual who has helped me in my quest to complete "No Fires In Tring" : you know who you are.

However, the book would not have been possible without the cast of engaging characters with whom I worked in Berkhamsted and those in the Hertfordshire Newspapers office and printing works in Hemel Hempstead.

The exceptions to the 'no naming' rule are: Gazette photographer Peter Ward and former chief Hemel Hempstead reporter Daphne Hughes who helped in my research; and works experts John Newberry and Mike Spittles and Mrs Jennifer Honour, daughter of the late works manager and director of the family-owned newspaper Lyonel Needham, who answered my plea for information about how the paper was printed.

And finally, thanks to my pal Paul Daniel, whose recollections of our journalism training were generally more accurate that my own.

Cover by Brian Young

Printed in Great Britain
by Amazon